SALT OF
THE EARTH

SALT OF THE EARTH

Walter Dirks

eagle

Bath, England

British Library Cataloguing in Publication Data. A Catalogue record for this book is available from the British Library.

Published by Eagle Publishing Ltd, 6 Kestrel House, Mill Street, Trowbridge, Wilts BA14 8BE.

Typesetting by Eagle Publishing Ltd
Printed and bound in Spain by BookPrint S.L., Barcelona
ISBN No. 0 86347 376 8

For further information and help visit the web site at www.saltoftheearth.org

CONTENTS

To Jesus,

the man who lived 2,000 years ago,

words can never express the gratitude

for all you have done

INTRODUCTION

This book is the result of about fifteen minutes thought back in the middle of 1997! At the time I was driving along the M5 motorway in England on my way to a photographic assignment when my mind was flooded with thoughts about producing a book. These thoughts had never occurred to me before, but the theme of 'changed lives' entered my mind and what really 'hit me' was that people's lives are still being changed, for the better, when they come to know a man who lived 2,000 years ago! In that short space of time I had the concept for a book that would illustrate how this could happen through 'portraits and personal stories' from around the world.

I was immediately excited with visions of world travel and meeting interesting people. Of course, I also thought about the practical implications such as funding, family support and leaving my commercial photography business relatively unattended for a year or two, to say nothing of my family! I decided to test the idea with my wife, some close friends and Bishop James Jones whom I had come to know through the church I attend in Bristol. I felt they were all honestly encouraging so decided to make a start. I had mixed feelings, no money and no publisher, but shortly after I photographed the first person I was offered help with the funding and later everything else fell into place. So began a journey that would take me around the world several times. Exciting? Yes! Little did I know that the biggest impact would come through photographing and interviewing the people in this book!

It is not intended to be a 'Who's Who' type of book. I decided who should be included through recommendation, research and introductions and I have been greatly moved, challenged and inspired by these people. It is very humbling to hear of the great loss experienced when someone close dies, or of a battle with alcohol and drugs. A few reached 'rock bottom' with no way forward and suicide a major consideration. Others lived a life with little love, joy or happiness. Some interviews were filled with laughter and others with tears as memories came to the surface, but in each individual I could clearly see a deep and life-sustaining peace that is hard to explain. Everyone was different but they all had the same spirit, and as they told their story I realised that I was encountering who had changed them. It was like walking into a room that has been rearranged by someone, and although you haven't physically seen the person who did the rearranging, you can have some knowledge of that person.

Some of the people in this book are enormously successful, like Michael Jones who, as an All Black, is recognised as one of the best rugby players ever! Others have been less successful, but without exception they give the glory to the author of their achievements and thank him for the miracle of a changed life. Each one would admit to not being perfect but they are all confident of their future and yes, sometimes there is a lot of kicking and screaming …we are, after all, only human!

The idea for this book may have taken only fifteen minutes of thought but it took many, many hours of work to produce. I have had much help and support from many dear friends and, because our own lives are not always as dramatic, we hope that in some way your life will be enriched through reading these stories.

Walter Dirks

I was born in Los Angeles to an Italian father and Syrian mother and had a devoutly Catholic upbringing – Catholic schools, Catholic churches, no meat on Fridays. Work-wise, at thirteen years old I was on stage for the first time, in the play *Oliver*. I had one line, 'What next is the question?' and I knew this was where I wanted to be for the rest of my life. It was the one thing that I could do twenty-fours hours a day, seven days a week, not get paid and yet be the happiest guy on the planet.

I entered university as a performing arts major and ended up with a degree in economics and law. I practiced criminal defence law for two years and remember one day sitting in my office just *hating* my professional life. A friend looked at me and said, 'Bruce, why don't you just go back to doing what you love to do?' So at twenty-six years of age I ended up back in the acting profession.

In 1983, I landed my first job. I had two lines in *Murder She Wrote* and I felt I had arrived! Through many years of very competitive struggle, and a few years of breathing room, I managed to eke out a living. By 1989 my career (and my life in general) really started taking off. I was teamed up with a beautiful young actress whom everybody in town wanted on their arm and was going from one television show to another, on a co-starring and guest starring level. I remember one day sitting in an easy chair with a beer in my hand and my dog next to me, watching myself on TV on three different shows in one evening. I was making good money and my life-long dreams were being fulfilled very quickly.

Suddenly everything went into a tailspin . . .

It all peaked in May and June 1989 but by July, it had fallen apart. The girl left me for another guy and, that distressed me so much emotionally, that suddenly everything went into a tailspin.

We had lived very high and very fast so there were no financial reserves at all. I found myself sleeping on a friend's sofa with nothing – and I mean, *NOTHING*. During that period of despair I went into the hills of Coldwater Canyon all alone in the middle of the day because I didn't have work, and looking out over Universal Studios in the distance I cried my eyes out. I looked up to heaven saying, 'Jesus, you've got to save me.' Somehow, through whatever education I'd received in Catholic school, church, and years of friends telling me about the Lord, those seeds had taken root. In that pit of despair, I knew that the only thing that was going to save me from going under completely was the Son of the Living God. I cried out to him and I *literally* gave him my life, all by myself, sitting in that park. It was something that had been explained to me many, many times, so I knew what to do, I knew the prayer to pray, sentence by sentence.

In 1991 I felt called to join a drama group travelling to Australia for six weeks to do missionary work, but the last thing in the world I wanted to do with my time was be a missionary. I was a very ambitious and competitive actor in an industry that's very much out of sight, out of mind; an industry that does not smile upon the word 'Christian'. Consequently, as I felt the Lord's call to join that ministry, my answer was 'No'!

And so began a struggle, a tooth and nail, scratch and kick, fight with the Lord for about two or three weeks. In my professional eyes, it was like career suicide, and I had worked too hard to throw everything away for six weeks of missionary work.

There's an African-American spiritual called 'You' arms too short to box with God'. In any event, I finally surrendered because I knew that God wanted me to do this thing and it was going to be a serious mistake to disobey. I joined the Drama Ministry and went to Australia kicking and screaming all the way. Sure enough, when I returned, my agent released me immediately. She said, 'Bruce, this Christian thing is getting in the way.' As a result, I found myself seriously struggling with God, shaking my fist at him, along the lines of 'So this is what I get for being a missionary? This is what I get for being obedient?'

About a year and a half after I returned from Australia, the leader of that missionary team phoned and said, 'Bruce, I received a letter today from South Africa. A director out there is making a new "Jesus" film and they're looking for a more down-to-earth, more real-looking Jesus. He wants a professional actor who loves the Lord, and I think you may want to give this guy a call.' Little did I know, the Lord did have plans for my life, plans for my good, when, to me at the time, they looked like plans for my harm. In November 1992, I found myself growing my hair and a beard and memorising every word spoken by Jesus as recorded by Matthew. In January 1993, I flew to South Africa for a frame-by-frame, scripture-by-scripture walk through the life of the greatest figure in universal history.

I could spend ten days telling you the discoveries I made in making *The Gospel According to Matthew*. It's a funny thing about Jesus, everybody just assumes they know who he was 2,000 years ago, exactly who he is today. As I began to walk through his life, I discovered that I too had just assumed. I had never before stopped and asked myself the question, 'Who was this man really, 2,000 years ago?' I know what religion tells me, I know how the greeting cards paint it, I know what the Renaissance paintings look like, but what's the *truth* here? For the purposes of *Matthew*, for the first time in my life, I had to stop everything I was doing and ask myself those questions.

I began to look at the Gospel, not so much searching for great spiritual truth, although I had to do that for purposes of the film as well, but more in terms of the practical events of the day. In acting we say that a man's heart is revealed in his actions – if you want to know who a man *is*, you look at what he *does* with his time, with his resources, what choices he makes, and therein is the first big discovery.

I'd never thought of it before — Jesus had a *choice*. I began to realise that if anybody had a choice in life it's the Son of the Living God. No one is telling him what to do. He's *choosing* all he does. So therefore, what was it *really* like that day he was coming down from the Sermon on the Mount, and the leper approached him? Jesus is undoubtedly exhausted from being up there preaching all day. He's been out in the elements with all the people, their babies, their camels and donkeys; his throat is strained and parched; he's covered with dust from the wind, surrounded by soul-hungry people and in the middle of all this he hears a voice, 'Lord, if you're willing, you can make me clean.' He is faced with a choice. What does he do? Does he choose to toss him a few bucks and just move on? Does he decide to pay attention to the pretty people or the fancy people? No, he stops everything he's doing for this guy whom everyone else despises, who had been kicked out of his house and the townspeople didn't want him living there any more. The Son of the Living God stops what he's doing *for that guy*. And I looked at that event and thought, My goodness! My goodness! What does that tell me about who this man was 2,000 years ago! About what is important to him? I read Psalm 139, and I paraphrase, 'I hand-formed you while you were yet in your mother's womb.' And it hit me, this man isn't just someone that's sick, it's not just some person that Jesus loves, he's literally *his creation*! I began to see that in my relationship with the Saviour I'm not just some sinner he loves. I'm his baby.

**I had never
before stopped
and asked myself
the question**

In the shoot, I had a big speech from Matthew Chapter 11: 'Woe to you, Korazin! Woe to you, Besthsaida! If the miracles that were performed in you had been performed in Tyre and Sidon, they would have repented. It will be better for Tyre and Sidon on the day of judgement than for you.' Jesus goes on to pit Sodom against Capernaum. 'But you will go down to the depths.' He said, 'It would be better on judgement day for Sodom than for you.' And I looked at that speech and thought, 'My goodness, these are some seriously harsh words.' If the words are taken out of context it removes them from a personality, they are just words, HARSH words. But when they are plugged into context and into the heart of Jesus, that's different! I was having a very hard time as an actor marrying the harshness of those words with the heart of the man I discovered. I didn't know how to do it. I didn't know how to say lovingly, 'You will go down to the depths.' I knew in my head that love was in there somewhere, but in my heart, I didn't know how to do it.

One of the things an actor really tries to latch onto is the character's viewpoint — what the world looks like through the character's eyes. I had yet to grasp deep down a sense of what the world looks like through the eyes of Jesus. It's something I'd never thought of before the film and as I talked to many people I discovered that very few people have ever really considered it. We just *assume* it looks to Jesus as it looks to us. But, I discovered that day that it doesn't.

I was standing with several hundred Moroccans who were playing the villagers of Korazin and Bethsaida. There were another hundred or so crewmembers and I paced back and forth across a focus line, desperately asking, 'Lord, show me what it all looks like through your eyes.' I wasn't seeking a vision or anything like that. I was trying to grasp a mindset; a vision was the last thing I had in mind. But what happened is very, very difficult to describe, it was just a billionth of a second, it was so quick. The experience was heartbreak — heartbreak like I never imagined heartbreak could be in a million heartbreaks. It was a depth of heartbreak unimaginable! What I 'saw' in my heart, was a reaction to a sea of people living lives in ways he didn't plan — living lives outside of his love, outside of his goodness, outside of his protection, just banging into each other, destroying their own lives, destroying everybody's life around them — all for lack of coming to him. To the human eye, to *my* eye, it just looked like normal life, but to him, it was so *tragically* short of the mark, so *horrific*. He knows the ideal and his reaction was heartbreak beyond heartbreak.

I remember a Scripture came to life and spoke in my heart . . . 'He had *compassion* on the crowds because they were helpless, like sheep without a shepherd.' — And it hit me that what I was experiencing was just a billionth of his *compassion* for people. — I remember exploding emotionally and weeping uncontrollably. — The Director came over to me, put his hand on my shoulder and he asked 'Are you OK?' — I looked up at him and all I could say was, 'It kills him, Reg. — It just kills him.' — His eyes welled up with tears; somehow, he understood what I was saying. — If there are a handful of days that changed my life *forever*, and I mean, forever, that one ranks No. 2 to salvation! — It goes back and forth with the day we filmed the Crucifixion. They go back and forth, — No. 2 with No. 3. No 1 — Salvation.

The Crucifixion was pain immeasurable. It was a trauma that couldn't be defined. It was hard beyond one's wildest imaginings. Isaiah 52 says that Jesus' face would be beaten and marred beyond recognition as a human being. The makeup artist went to work on me for a couple of hours and when we came out, I could see the reaction in people's faces around me — recoiling in *horror* at the sight of me — someone screaming for help because they thought I'd been in a terrible accident. I'll never forget the *shame* that came over me. I'd never thought of Jesus feeling shame, but that day I felt the shame of having people look at me like that.

What happened is very, very difficult to describe, it was just a billionth of a second

I remember arriving on the set and walking through the crowd of people who had become my friends. There were a couple of hundred people up on that hill and not one of them said a word to me. They set up a little chair for me behind all the work, and left me in that chair alone, away from everybody. I felt, 'Hey, look at me, do you want to talk to me?' They didn't want to deal with me at all! Morocco is an Islamic country, and a group of female extras started weeping and wailing at the sight of me — I can't explain the emotion! As I sat in the chair, I felt something on my left hand. One of my eyes was glued shut and the other one was glued open — I turned my head to see what was on my hand. A little Moroccan girl of about twelve years old was standing there holding my hand as tears streamed down my face. She couldn't communicate with me because she couldn't speak English — she was just reaching out to me in the only way that she knew how. And I'll never forget what she meant to me in my personal sense of aloneness that day. Just the human touch. She held my hand for about twenty minutes. Then they finally began filming and I had to go.

It's one thing to have a person spit in your face; it's one thing to be whipped, but to have your own *child* grab that whip! It's one thing to be lied about, but to have your own *child* look you in the face! It's one thing to have someone say, 'Crucify him,' but to have y*our own child* make that choice. I tremble to think of his heartbreak. His whole life was lived for these people and unto them — and all they could do was spit in his face. The tragedy, the pain . . . the *pain* is off the meter.

I'll never forget what she meant to me . . .

We tend to think about the physical pain, but *that* was *nothing* compared to all these things going on in the emotions, in the spirit, in the mind. At several points during the day it became very rough for me physically and people approached me and said, 'Hey, Bruce, you know, you don't *have* to do this stunt. We can get somebody to do it.' But I chose to do it myself. Why? Because I'm crazed! I don't know! But in making that choice, for the first time in my life it hit me that he had the same choice. I think of the man who says, 'If you're the Son of God, why don't you come down off the cross?' And I suddenly realised as we were doing that scene that he could have. He had the power of heaven and earth at his fingertips. He could have snapped his fingers and said, 'Forget it. These people aren't worth it.'

I remember hanging on that cross, the aloneness, and the sense of going through something that no one can share. I stood on a platform with two leather straps on either side of the crossbeam. I jammed my hands into those straps and to get a sense of reality of the straining of the arms, neck and joints, when the director called 'Action', I kicked the platform out from under me and literally hung. My feet dangled free. I remember just counting the seconds, the physical trauma involved, just counting the seconds until the Director yelled, 'Cut'! It got very, very late in the day, the sun was sinking, and we had to shoot the death shot. The Director was on scaffolding to my left and we did Take 1. My face fell to the right and he said, 'OK, we've got to do a second take.' He began to give instructions to the crew and as I rolled my head around to look at him, he looked into my face and stopped. He stopped dead. I remember his eyes welled up with tears and he said, 'That's it.' He pointed to the crew and told them, 'Get him down. We're done.' I mumbled to him through the blood in my teeth, because I'd been pretty knocked around all day along, 'I can do it again,' and he said, 'No, we're *done*. That's it. Get him down.' And that was it. The day was done.

A couple of weeks later he and I were sitting in a little coffee shop and I asked, 'What did you see when you looked at me that made you stop it like that?' He looked at me again very seriously and said, 'I saw a man dying'!

Jesus! Jesus! The reality of who he is. That was his ultimate representation of himself as God. He was never more God. It's a funny thing, we tend to think of the resurrection as his greatest moment of 'Godness'. I'm no theologian but I tend to think it was the *cross*. His ultimate act was giving his life for you and me. He's God. He's *big*. The resurrection was easy stuff! I think of a Father God sitting there and he has a choice, to save his own Son, or to save *you and me*. And he literally turns his back on his only Son! What parent would make that kind of choice? It's love *immeasurable*. Beyond comprehension.

Our presentation of Jesus was obviously very different from anything that's ever been done before. Jesus is presented as a man of joy as opposed to a solemn mystic and that has been a revelation to a lot of people. It's changed a lot of non-believers into believers and it has released goodness into people's lives on every level. We never set out to change the image of Jesus for the world. The director and I were just so scared to make a mistake. We found ourselves on our knees, begging God to do something. My constant prayer was, 'Lord make me a puppet on your string.' I didn't want to say a word; I didn't want to make a move that wasn't him.

The Lord began to show us things. He led us to Hebrews 1:9 where it says that he was anointed with the oil of joy above his brethren. He began to show me compassion with a new understanding. Passion like I never knew passion. Love beyond love. And he began to show me that he wanted me to incorporate that into what I was doing on camera. That these things were essential to his character and his personality, and the rest is history. In every way, my life is *dramatically* changed.

In terms of activity, ninety per cent of what I do now is ministry. Sometimes I'm in a tent in the middle of rural Africa, talking about Jesus with people who don't even have shoes. Recently I was in South Africa spending day after day going into High Schools and seeing droves of kids give their lives to Jesus. This is how I'm spending my day! I'll go back to my hotel room, turn on the TV, and see someone that I was with in acting class, and now he has his own television series and he's a big star.

I have a *passion* for making movies — I love it — but for the first time in my life I find myself honestly praying 'Lord, here am I — anything, *anything*. If I never make another movie in my life, let me walk in your service for the rest of my life. I don't care what it is, that's what I want to do.' This is the same person who, a few years ago, fought with God about six weeks in Australia on a missions trip!

Through the movie, I've come to a profound understanding of what's important in life. It's not me. It's not making movies. That's fun. But what is important is other people. I have come into an understanding of who he is and who he wants me to be. I've come to realise that he is the model and that *giving* is the key to everything. It's the key to everything that *he* did. We kick and scream when God asks us to turn left or turn right. We kick and scream to drop an extra five bucks in the collection plate or, like me, not wanting to go to Australia! But my goodness Jesus gave his *life* for *me*. I mean — whew! He gave his *life*, for crying out loud! When are we ever going to get that? Hopefully on some level, I'm starting to understand it.

What parent would make that kind of choice?

SULLY PAEA
MAKING A DIFFERENCE

I was born in 1951 on a beautiful little island in the South Pacific, but in my mum's terms, I was 'an accident'.

When I was two-and-a-half years old my mum, who was no longer with my father, sent me to live with my great-uncle. I really couldn't understand why I was taken away and even yet it has not been explained. My assumption was that my stepfather didn't want me around because he was starting a new family.

My great uncle brought me up in the way islanders have been living for centuries. He taught me survival skills like fishing, hunting and understanding the sea, so I'm a survivor, but he was a very hard man and abused me. Because I felt mistreated, I became rebellious and when I was nine or ten I left school and joined up with the wrong crowd.

I eventually started work as an apprentice motor mechanic and at eighteen moved to New Zealand with my grandfather. Although I had a lot of dreams and desires, things I wanted to do in life, they never really seemed to happen because I was in a family where alcohol was in control. We spent all our time in the pub, drinking and more drinking, until I became an alcoholic myself. That led me into trouble and I became involved in the gangland scene of drugs and violence. I had a good job, earned decent money, but all of it went into supporting my habits. I played in a band and sometimes we would go and play in a club and have a great time, but I would return to my room by myself and the loneliness would settle in again. I drank to drive that loneliness away; that was my lifestyle for quite a long time.

I became totally lost and depressed and began to look for some answers. I tried church, but the church I attended was full of people whom I viewed as hypocrites because they were drunk the night before. We all drank together, and they acted as if they were holy on Sunday, but the rest of the week, they did what they wanted. That didn't make sense to me. I felt life and Christianity must be more than that.

On the day I hit rock bottom and felt I had nothing to live for, I began to call out to God. I said, 'Do something, otherwise I'm going to kill myself.' I seemed to come up against a brick wall, but an aunt who was attending a Pentecostal church rang me and asked if I was interested in going with her. I didn't really want to go, but as I had nothing to do that evening I decided to tag along.

That was my first real encounter with Christianity. I saw and felt something in that church and in the young people there that I had never experienced before — the joy on their faces, the expression of love, everything packed into one. I felt at peace, but at the same time, I felt lost. The church was just an ordinary Pentecostal church and I was all dressed up, suit, tie; I was probably the only one dressed up there but I was miserable inside. I felt they had something that I didn't have so I told my aunt that I would like to go back the following Sunday and find out more.

During that week, I lived in hell and drank almost continually. My whole life was in turmoil, but I was determined to find out what those young people had. I went back and was challenged. They sang a song, in the middle of which they paused, and one young person read out the verse John 3:16, 'For God so loved the world that he gave his one and only Son, that whoever believes in him shall not perish but have eternal life.' A simple verse from the Bible, but it hit me so hard that I left there shaking.

Do something, otherwise I'm going to kill myself

About 2.00 am the following morning I had a dream in which I saw about twenty young people from church singing the song. All except one of the singers received God's blessing. I said to a person in the dream, 'Who is the one without the blessing?' The person replied, 'It's you!'

I woke up scared and sweating because the room was filled with demonic things. I knew, because it was part of my culture. It was a pitch-black night and it felt as if these things were calling to me. Out of frustration I got on my knees and cried out to God, 'If there is a God, and if you are who you say you are, *do something for me*, because this is the end of the road for me. I have nothing else to live for.'

For the very first time I felt the presence of God: something good came in, lifted the clouds of darkness, and banished them. It was as if a great big light came into that room and took the load that I had been carrying all my life off me. I cried, and with the tears he took away the hatred, the rejection, the loneliness, and the empty feeling, totally!

In the morning, I rang my aunt and told her what had happened. I couldn't wait to get back to church. The next Sunday I heard the gospel loud and clear and it hit me again so I committed my life to God. It was wintertime and it was cold. When they asked me if I wanted to be baptised I said, 'I want everything that God has to give me!' I jumped into the water with all my clothes on and when I got out, soaking wet, I drove off to my family to tell them what had happened. They looked at me as if I was drunk, or had gone nuts!

From then on my whole lifestyle changed. My aunt was so helpful and was right there for me as a young Christian. When I gave my heart to the Lord, I left everything. Everything! My band, my girlfriend, I left the lot. I said, 'God, I want you more than anything else.' The other band members were wondering what had happened to me as I left all my musical equipment and records. I told them I had found something better. They weren't very happy about that! I experienced persecution from my family and friends. I had been a party animal whom everybody enjoyed being around. I could sing, play guitar, and liven up the parties, and now there was none of that.

The friends, with whom I used to drink walked in the opposite direction when they saw me coming. They just didn't want to know. It seemed that the light that was in me was shining out to them, but it was too bright, and they would shy away. I was concerned but decided I would rather lose my friends than lose what I knew was more valuable than anything I had ever had. The peace that I'd been looking for, for such a long time, I had found! There was no way I would go back to the evil and demonic of the past; I just wanted this new life! I told God to take me and do whatever he liked with me. I guess because I was sincere, God took me and wiped the slate clean.

I had found my way out of a world that was full of people going to hell but what was I going to do about the others? That haunted me for a long time and finally from that desire, my community work was born.

A friend suggested that I might want to go to Bible College. I said, 'If it will help me to prepare for whatever God has in store for me, I will do it.' So in 1975 with their support and encouragement I went to the Nazarene Theological College in Brisbane and studied for three years.

That was a big change for me, particularly with my limited educational background. There God dealt with the whole of my character in-depth. I enjoyed myself in Brisbane so much that I didn't want to come back. I said to God, 'Take me anywhere in the world, but don't take me to Otara,' — the area in which I had been living. But he told me, 'Go back to New Zealand.' So I said, 'God, if I am to go back to New Zealand, I want two things. I want a place for a Drop-In Centre and I want a big house so that I can take in kids.'

They looked at me as if I was drunk, or had gone nuts!

Within six months God gave me both those things. My place and the Drop-In Centre became a local hangout. I felt that the local churches were somehow distant from the community so I began to seek direction and God clearly said to me, 'Get out there, and make a change. Make a difference.' I took the step of faith, with no money. I was invited by Youth for Christ to sing in a prison where I shared my plans with the prisoners. After the service, one of them, a recent Christian, said 'I'd like to help you out financially because I believe in what you are doing.' He gave his life savings — $600.00. It was everything he had!

Around that time, I met a lovely Canadian girl called Joanne who was with a group of students from a Bible College running a holiday programme for kids in the park near us and we just clicked. I knew she was the one so I travelled to Canada to meet her family. We decided to marry and live in New Zealand, after which we started straight into the youth work and didn't have a honeymoon, so heaven is going to be our honeymoon!

Over several years, we built up the ministry into quite a large organisation and turned it into a Government-sponsored work scheme, which just grew and grew. Eventually I left that project because the people who were supposed to be helping me were very money-orientated. I'm people-orientated and didn't focus on the money, so they came in and took over the whole work. After that the place fell apart, together with all the work that had been built up. I was very disappointed.

My life from then on involved much searching and God took me the long way round. I went into a Food Bar and Fruit Shop business on my own in Otara. At weekends, I was still involved in working with youth; during school holidays we ran activities, and when the kids came in, we would feed them.

In 1988 we took a break and went to Christchurch for two and a half years and I believe God took us there for a period of restoration and healing. Even there I was still involved with youth — I just don't seem to be able to get away from that. God taught me so much, particularly about faith and trust. He stripped me of my pride and everything I had so that I had to depend *totally* on him. He shut every door and I couldn't find work; I'd never had any problem with that before. I've always been one to create my own work if I've needed to, but every door remained firmly shut, to a point where I was really desperate. All I could hear was God saying to me, 'Be still, and know that I am God.' When we returned to Otara we had nothing, and had to start all over again but God had taken me on a path of learning and most of all, of discovering myself. I came back with new confidence, a fresh vision, and zeal.

In 1993 a little seed was planted for the place we now have, and it gradually grew from a small group at the back of my house into our youth centre called Crosspower. People in Otara lack education and high unemployment brings poverty, which leads to crime and many other issues, which in turn leads to unemployment, and so the circle continues. God has given Christians answers to these problems, but we become so isolated within our churches that we don't know how to begin to communicate or meet the needs of the people. I believe that God wants us to make a difference in people's lives.

We work closely with the schools, the police, the welfare system, and the youth justice and community correction department. We create an environment where young people want to be, where they want to do things and where they want to learn. Most of them have learning disabilities. We also work with kids who have been kicked out of school because they don't fit. I've found that a lot of them are creative and need to be in a different learning environment. I came out of that scene — I hated sitting in a classroom and listening to a teacher speaking, because half the time I didn't understand what was being said. But in a workshop where there

Every door remained firmly shut . . . I was really desperate

were tools and machinery, I thrived. The majority of these children can't read or write so we teach them the basics and give them hands-on experience of stripping down machines, fixing bikes and woodcarving. It's a slow process because first we have to earn their respect but we want them to take some skills with them when they move on.

We have a monthly Friday night café and sleepovers during the weekends when kids come in and do fun things. They are amazed — the bikes, the gym that we made out of scrap metal, the music — they go wild on Friday and Saturday nights and they go to church on Sunday. We have no problem bringing in the gospel because everybody knows that Crosspower is a church-based spiritual place. At first, we didn't have a good church connection. It was only after a change of pastors that I began to realise that our work needed support. For some time now the church has been very supportive of what we are doing and we have a good working relationship with the pastor and his team.

We run a camp and take the kids into the countryside where we see a completely different group. Their attitudes change, their whole life changes. We find we can communicate very well with them there and many have made commitments. They find it easier away from their friends and peers where there's no pressure. Out in the open air with nature, they can see God much more clearly.

I need to be creative in my work and my creativity comes in when I'm communicating with God. When I'm just by myself, sitting in peace and quietness, reading the Word, God teaches me things. I like it that way. Where we live is very country-like, and I spend a lot of time just being out in the open, breathing the fresh air and talking to God. This is where my spiritual strength comes from. It also comes from seeing people change, seeing lives transformed, seeing people like Daniel, Walter, Bonny and others come through, and seeing them develop into leaders. Walter works with the hard core. Guys between twelve and fifteen years of age who don't think twice about picking up a knife and robbing a shop. Many of them have made a commitment to the Lord, but Walter has continued to live and work with them.

I have been asked how can we handle all these kids. The ones I'm working with now are a lot harder than ten or fifteen years ago. There is no respect, due to a lack of love and attention from the home, where the parents are either working or there are no parents at all, so the kids learn to fend for themselves and turn to crime. I know I need to be more like Christ to them, in patience and love. Every now and again, some kid will come in and really push me to the maximum. To handle it, I just disappear to pray and ask God for more love. In looking back I can say that there is no way, with my background and little education that I could have achieved what I have without God. I give him all the glory.

My wife Joanne has always been supportive and God has blessed us with three beautiful kids. We all play music together and they have become leaders in their own way. God has led some beautiful people across my path and they are my thermostat, they let me know when I am under stress. Our board is very committed — so I'm blessed!

God has supplied our needs and last year an interesting thing happened. We were talking about staff members' dreams and I said that my dream was to own a Harley because I had been a biker, and once a biker, always a biker! Half an hour later, a guy turned up and we talked about motorcycles. He said he had one for sale and about two hours later, I'd got the Harley . . . for nothing! On another occasion my wife needed to go to Canada to see her family because her grandparents hadn't got long to live. Somebody blessed her and three of them went and their fares were paid for, there and back. We've just had so much. I feel like a millionaire.

A guy turned up and we talked about motorcycles . . .

I have found in my own personal life the importance of being available. So many kids have commented, 'One thing that we have found with you is that you are always here.' It gives them confidence. They know that if they have a need I'm available, and they can get wise advice. If they need direction and don't know what to do they come to us knowing that they can get some answers. I don't have all the answers but sometimes, just being here as their sounding board when they need to talk is sufficient. I've talked to many people who have said, 'I don't know why I'm telling you this, but I feel released,' and I tell them that's what it's all about. Half the time I don't even remember what they were telling me but just listening has given me the right to be able to speak to their lives and say, 'You need to do something about this. You need to let go of some of this. You need to burn your past bridges, look at where you are now and build on the bridge of the future, to cross over to the future. Destroy the past, literally bury it.' I don't know how many people I have spoken to with regard to blowing up bridges. A lot don't burn their bridges and they continue with life still carrying the hurts, the frustrations, the things they have been carrying with them all their lives, and never really let go of them. Just recently, I've had some workers through here who know that God had called them here for a purpose but they didn't last the distance, and that is simply because their past caught up with them and they ended up having to move on. So I use this illustration all the time. This is where you are. That is where you've been. Look back and work out things that haven't been dealt with, because you're not going to be able to cross that bridge to the future without blowing up the bridge of the past. At the same time, a lot have come back and thanked me for taking the time to tell them.

Our overall vision is to infiltrate and touch every corner of our community, particularly in corners where it's at risk or corners where there is a lot of drug activity. We've already dealt with one area where there were a lot of drugs, alcohol, violence, graffiti, etc. The local council asked if we would like to run a project there and we took the opportunity. We've been there for two years now and the place has completely changed. We put in play equipment for kids and developed the area so it has become a safer street for people to live in. All the gang involvement has moved on and it is now a very safe little corner for families. That's our vision. We want to change our community to make it a comfortable place where people can live safely.

Having been involved in the community for a long time, we noticed that the age when kids are getting into trouble is getting younger and younger. We used to deal with the twelve- to fifteen-year-olds. Now it's gone down to the five to eight-year-olds. We decided to nip the problem in the bud and now go into the primary schools twice a week, working with the Principal and a number of the teachers. They identify the kids who are at risk, the ones who have the tendency to get into trouble, and are involved in bullying and negative behaviour. Two of our workers during the lunch-hour mix and mingle, have lunch with the kids and develop a good relationship with them. After hours they either bring them to our centre or join them in the after-school activities, just being like a big brother or sister, helping develop character behaviour and teaching them how to relate to other kids. If there are big issues that they can't handle they come to me, but most of the time they work with the kids where they are. We try to deal with crime prevention, and also building the bridges because with some of the kids, their negative behaviour can be due to something deep-seated that they haven't been able to share.

Because many of the problems start at home we focus on working with either mum or dad. In the majority of cases the kids come from single parent homes and so, if it's Dad, I'll work with him or, if it's Mum, the ladies can work with her. Recently a nine- and ten-year-old were suspended from school for bullying. They don't want them back. If the problem is not dealt with

I don't know how many people I have spoken to with regard to blowing up bridges

at that level, by the time they reach twelve or thirteen, they're already streetwise, prospective gang material, and their lives will develop from there into the drug scene. The drug dealers use the younger ones to sell their drugs. So we step in and work with the parents, the majority of whom are happy with our involvement. They want the best for their kids. They want help and sometimes they don't know where to turn to get it although some don't recognise that there is a problem. They don't want their kids to get into trouble, but they mix with the wrong crowd, and peer pressure makes them continue.

A lot of kids whom I don't know say, 'My dad knows you!' And when they tell me his name I think, 'Oh yes. I remember him when he was , . . !' Makes me feel old! But because they know my track record, it gives the parents confidence that their kids are in a safe place and they will contact me if there is a problem. That's the advantage of being here so long and also seeing the changes.

Part of the community see us as youth, because of my connection with youth in the past. When I see someone on the street the first question is, 'How's the gym?' I like people knowing us like that. Even some church people know us in that way. When we were having church here people came freely because they knew it as the gym; it wasn't a church building. It's a different environment, a more comfortable place to be. It has developed over the years, from focusing mainly on youth to getting into the home, working more with parents and developing parental life skills, particularly with young mothers. But the gym is also used as a way of stress release for some, anger management, channelling all that negative energy into lifting weights or punching a punching bag. It's a way of releasing tension, a therapy.

We are doing what Jesus says, going out and making disciples, making a difference. Some churches isolate themselves and the gap between the church and the community has become so wide, but we are more like a springboard into the church. We have found that the kids with whom we work go freely into church now, because they are used to it here. This is a step in — they come here, they gain confidence, they get saved, and now they can go freely into church, whereas trying to bring them straight from the community into the church, they will think up about 200 excuses before they come — they just don't fit in. I came out of the church scene from a church organisation and know they are so far removed that it's very difficult to bring youth, or anybody to church. There has to be something in between to ease them in slowly, and this is where we are. We become the bridge.

They will think up about 200 excuses before they come

JANET MUSEVENI

I thought I knew everything there was to know about the Lord! Both my parents were committed Christians so I had heard about God and the work he could do in people's lives right from my very early childhood.

I attended church on Sundays but that was the extent of the Christian life I led and basically, my life belonged to me. I believed in myself and I didn't want anyone else involved. What I could do, I would do; what I couldn't, I wouldn't blame anybody else for. I really didn't have a relationship, or even much knowledge of God for myself. What I knew was what I had received from my mother and father, the church, etc, and it remained once removed. It wasn't within me.

When I was about eighteen years old, I lost my only brother and that was a very traumatic experience. My mother loved God very much, and I can remember telling her that I didn't want to know a God who could do this to her. She said, 'Don't say things like that about God. I can't believe that a child of mine can say such things.' I replied, 'I don't care what you think or what you say. I will never have anything to do with God in my life!' And from then on, I proceeded to live my life my way.

Growing up, I went to the primary school in our village and then to a nearby secondary school but before I could finish my schooling, my family had to leave Uganda because of the political problems. A cousin, who held a responsible position, was in conflict with the Government so we had to leave.

We went to Kenya to live for some time and it was there that I met my husband. He was someone I knew from way back because our families had been close and I had even been at the same school as him. He was living in Tanzania at that time, because he had also run away from Uganda. We got to know each other again and then married about three years after that in 1973.

Life in Tanzania was very difficult because we were living as refugees. My husband was quite involved in the resistance war against Idi Amin and because he travelled a lot of the time I had to bring up our children on my own. When my mother died, we couldn't even get back to Uganda for her funeral.

We came back in 1979 after the regime of Idi Amin had been overthrown. My husband was appointed Minister of Defence and decreed that he would fight anyone who tried to gain power without being elected by the people. The Government was trying to bring some stability to the country and have an election, but nothing seemed to work. When it rigged the elections and appointed itself, my husband went into the bush to fight. For two years we had tried to make a proper home and our children had started school, but once again I had to flee the country.

At that time we had four children, our last daughter being born in Uganda. Leaving the country was not something I wanted, but I had to go for their sake. We lived in Kenya for a very short period and then were told we had to find somewhere further away because the Ugandan Government was looking for us. It was quite traumatic because we only had two days' notice. I didn't know where in the world I was supposed to go and because I had the children with me, it was *very* difficult. I had a friend who was working in Kenya who tried to get a country that would agree to take us, and eventually she managed to get Sweden to accept us. It was imperative that we left so I packed one bag for my children and myself.

On arrival in Sweden, we were taken into a camp where political refugees lived and every

I can't believe that a child of mine can say such things

family was given a cottage. Ours was waiting for us, a small, warm house (and this was a very, *very* cold winter in Sweden) with beds made up and food in the fridge. Everybody was so kind to us. That night my children were asleep in their bedroom and I can remember sitting there, writing to my husband, not knowing whether he would receive my letter. I said, 'There must be a God in the world because here we are in a country of which we have no knowledge, and my children are sound asleep. They are comfortable, they've been fed and we are in a warm home — *there must be a God.*' This was in November and I told God that I would give him the gift of my heart that Christmas. I wrote to my husband again at Christmas and said that I had accepted the Lord. I walked with him for some time, but I wasn't totally committed because I hadn't got to know him and I only believed because of what I had experienced.

Three years later we were given an apartment in another town and our children went to school, as did I, to learn Swedish. One day in 1985 our front door bell rang and my daughter ran to open the door. She shouted! We all went to see what was the matter, and there was her father! We were overwhelmed because we were not expecting him. He had lost a lot of weight and he looked very different, but we were so grateful to see him again.

After the Ugandan Government fell we returned to find that many of our people had died. Most of what we knew was destroyed and the country looked abandoned. It was a traumatic experience and we didn't know where to begin. I visited places they called Reception Centres where they put children who were found walking by the roadside and had no families. There were many houses like that. I can remember going to one such centre where I found a group of some fifty children, some of them were half naked, the others clothed in rags, on a concrete floor, with nothing in the house, no furniture, no beds, no blankets, no lights, *no nothing*!

I told them what I had seen and showed them pictures

I stood there and cried, and said, 'Who is going to take care of these children? Where do we begin?' My husband was struggling to form a Government out of practically nothing, and I knew we could not wait for enough resources to do something for these children. I called a women's meeting and many turned up. I told them what I had seen and showed them pictures we had taken. I said we should be thankful we were alive, well and able to look after our own families, but we couldn't just ignore the poor children who really belonged to us as well. The women amazed me because from that day they began bringing food from their own houses to those children, sitting down and eating with them, bringing mattresses, blankets and everything they needed and that's how we started the orphanages.

When the work began I wondered how we would continue. I had questions in my heart on whether I was doing the best for my family. I also wondered if the experience I gained as an individual in my own family could help me with what I wanted to do on a national level. There were many unanswered questions and problems.

Around that time, Mrs Daisy Osborne came on an evangelical mission. Having heard what I was doing with the children, she sent me a note and some helpful books. I read in one of them: 'If you want to commit your life to the Lord, just pray this prayer.' I prayed the prayer and for some reason it touched my heart and I couldn't forget it. Later on I knelt down and said to the Lord, 'I want to pray a personal prayer to find out whether you are the God I hear about. This is our first Christmas in this country after so many years and it is very important for my family and for me. If you answer my prayer, I will know that you are God, and I want you to answer it before Christmas.' I left it at that. On Christmas Day around lunchtime I remembered my prayer and it had been answered exactly as I had asked. One side of me believed there was a God. After all I had only prayed that prayer to God and what I prayed for had happened. Then the other side of me said, 'Oh, come on. That's just a coincidence. It would have happened anyway!' I went to my room, knelt down again, and said to God, 'I am going to pray again just to confirm that you are the one. If you answer my prayer again, I will believe that you are God!' I prayed another personal prayer and again he answered. From that day on, I have never stopped praying!

I was amazed to find that God does exist, and that I had wasted so much time trying to live my life my way. God was there and he had been waiting for me all that time. When growing up and hearing the messages about God I blamed everyone I could think of for making him seem so judgemental. I was burdened and felt I must tell our children and the people that he is kind, that he's waiting and he's there. So I prayed and told as many people as I could about the Lord and his love and how he can change lives and make them meaningful. I started praying for the orphans, the young people, the families, the single mothers and all the work I was involved with. I started seeing miracles, God acting every day, bringing people together and finding us the help we needed.

From that first day, I have never stopped talking about the Lord. Since I have known him I have wondered every day just what I would have done without him. The responsibility I have in society brings more burdens and I know, because of him, many things have become much easier. I prayed that my children would come to know him earlier than I did and he was so gracious. They all know him so well and so confidently and they talk about him, because they have come to know him as their Saviour and Friend. He has been a wonderful mother and father to them because many times when we are not there for them, he is there and they are stronger and more confident because of that relationship.

I am sorry that I became a Christian after my mother died, because I understand so much more of what she used to tell me. My father died when I was very young, so I lived much of my life only with my mother. She was a very strong woman, and I couldn't understand where her strength came from. For instance, she used to go for fellowship with other Christians to a church that was about three miles from home. Sometimes she would come home on her own, late at night, and that was not something women did. We would go to meet her with a lamp and find her singing and praising the Lord. I could not understand why she was never frightened of anything. When I became a Christian I understood just what had given her the peace of mind, strength and confidence, and I wish she were still alive so that we could share that.

Since my husband became President of Uganda I don't know whether my life has changed that much, except of course, that more people look to me for help and support in different ways. Sometimes this can be burdensome because although I really want to help, as much as possible, on occasions it is just not practicable. My relationship with the Lord helps me even when I can't help materially. I give counselling and many times I find that actually helps more because it gives people strength to start finding solutions. I am in a position where I can be useful to many more people than if I were not here, but it is a big challenge and requires guidance from God.

When I fled from Uganda, I hadn't finished my education. The important thing then was survival and looking after my family, but I really wanted to complete my schooling because I felt it would help me to do better work. I started studying again and found that it influenced many women in this country to do the same.

The wife of a Head of State does not have to do *anything* if she doesn't want to! Whatever she undertakes depends on her heart, what she likes doing most. I thank God that he has given me a chance to contribute in a small way to the building of my country. Prayer is the focus of my life and I pray for Uganda *all the time*. I ask the Lord to make it his flagship and use it in the Continent of Africa as a *starting point* for him to shine.

I was burdened and felt I must tell . . .

GENERAL VYCHESLAV BORISOV

FAITH IN GOD IS IMPOSSIBLE TO DESTROY

I was born on 30th June 1939 in the town of Ramasgrin about 20 miles from Moscow. My mother worked throughout World War II as a nurse in a hospital, and my father, who was fighting in the war for Russia, was killed. I have no memory of him but I can remember it being a very hard time.

After the war, there was a famine so I became grateful for every piece of bread, and an apple for New Year's Eve was a great treat. Every time we had a holiday or free time off school, I would work to pay for books and shoes for the next year. I really appreciated those shoes and was very disappointed when they wore out. Childhood was tough and my life, like that of so many other poor people, consisted of working all hours for little or no money.

I was fortunate because I met some people who helped me to get a place at a Military College. It was one of the Suvorov Colleges. Alexander Suvorov was one of the greatest Russian Army Field Marshals and had never lost a battle. In his memory, Stalin started fifty colleges especially for war orphans, the idea being that they would be trained up to form a military Elite for the Russian Army. The College I attended was in Kiev and was a typical army barracks with strict discipline and routines.

In one of the combat operations my helicopter was hit

One year on vacation at a place where young people got together I met a beautiful girl. I asked her to dance with me and when she discovered that I was a cadet and a future officer she was already mine! We went out for three years — largely by correspondence because we were living a thousand miles or so apart! We were very much in love. I was still at college when we married, and we are still together after forty years.

I graduated from college with Honours and decided to go for my officer training at the Kremlin College, which is similar to West Point in America. In fact, today the colleges have become good friends and exchange students. I studied there for three years, instead of four, because I was working so hard, and graduated with a Gold Medal.

Following that I was stationed in many different parts of Russia before attending a Military Academy, which prepared high ranked officers for regiments and divisions. After a few years' experience in Soviet Germany I became the youngest Commander of a Division in the Infantry since World War II.

When the war in Afghanistan broke out I was sent there as Deputy Chief Commander of all Soviet combat troops. I took part in military action and in one of the combat operations my helicopter was hit by enemy fire. With my helicopter on fire and crashing to the ground, I cried out to the Lord. I knew that he was the only one who could hear me or help in that situation, because there was nothing in this world that could save me. After my helicopter hit the ground, I opened my eyes and saw all my colleagues around me. Dead. I was lying on the ground. I could see the mountains. I was still alive! At that moment, everything in me was changed irrevocably. The Lord God heard the cry of my soul and gave me back my life.

This tragedy happened in on 11th July 1984* and was the turning point of my life because I came to believe that the Lord God exists. I knew about belief in God and of course I had visited churches and spent a little time studying, but I was an atheist and considered all this with the negative objective of criticising and disproving. It was part of my programme as a Commander — we had to learn how to resist and criticise such beliefs in case we found them in our soldiers.

GENERAL VYCHESLAV BORISOV

This was the very first time in the history of the Soviet Union

Marx had taught us that religion was the opiate of the people. I was a Communist, raised to believe that anybody who didn't believe in Communism was my enemy and must be destroyed. As a result, in the army I had persecuted soldiers who were believers and my task was to change their minds and make them non-believers again. In order to achieve this I tried to convince them by many different means, through physical influence, through persecution by taking their rights away, or sending them to prison, or some other equally awful places.

All of them, every time, said, 'General Borisov, the Lord God does exist. You must believe in him. If something awful happens to you down here, Marx and Lenin will not help you, only the Lord God, our Heavenly Father; he who loves all of us, and only he, can come and rescue you. Believe in him, and cry out to him, and then you will find you are blessed in this life, and in the next.' I just laughed at them. However, when I was suddenly confronted by death in the helicopter crash I only had one thought — perhaps God can save me now. In the few moments left, I cried out to him.

I was taken from the scene of the crash to a hospital and spent a long time in intensive care. The doctors nearly gave up on me because they thought I would be severely handicapped and would probably not survive. I knew nothing about prayer at that time but I prayed day and night as best I could. I had never heard people praying before and had never held a Bible. At that time, if someone had seen me reading a Bible or if I had mentioned God just once in conversation, the KGB would have come to get me the same day and I would have lost my job and been put into prison.

I prayed a lot to the Lord and asked him many things. I asked him to finish the war and get the soldiers back home to their families. I was amazed that the Lord answered my prayers — *literally*. I'm absolutely astounded how great and wonderful the Lord God is, how powerful and strong he is and how much he loves us. Now I can see how misled we were; Lenin and Marx have long disappeared. They lied to the people and were responsible for the destruction of many. Millions are still reaping the fruits of Communism and have suffered greatly. However, Jesus Christ, praise God, is alive and will live forever.

Every day after my crash, something would happen to strengthen my faith and understanding. My disadvantage was that I knew very little about God and hadn't read the Bible. I hadn't listened to preachers and I had no Christian study material but thanks to God I eventually recovered and in 1991** when Rev Cecil Todd of Revival Fires came to my military base and asked to preach, I invited him in. This was the very first time in the history of the Soviet Union that a military General had allowed an American preacher onto his base!

After hearing his message I was shocked, because I had never heard anyone speak of Jesus the way he did. I think God pushed me to allow them in, but afterwards many thousands of Russian soldiers converted to Christianity and all of us were given Bibles. I was almost afraid to take one because to have such a book was a very dangerous thing then.

Paul Kim, a Korean American, who had a church in Moscow, then came to preach every week on my military base and every Sunday we visited his church. I was exploring something totally new and wanted to know more about God. I joined his Seminary, studied there for two years, and found there were so many others all around the world who believed the same as I did and that the way was available to everyone.

In our Communist, closed-up system we had been living isolated desert-type lives knowing nothing about God's grace and his mercy. Unfortunately, even now, Russia is living in this desert and needs the living water of the Lord.

Because there have been many years of terror through killings, oppression, and persecution, many families know nothing about God, but the Russian people are strong and faith in the Lord God is impossible to destroy completely.

By using my command, over 1 million Red Army soldiers have now received Bibles provided by Revival Fires. I retired from my position in the Army in 1996 and I now go into schools and prisons, handing out Bibles, and telling people about the Lord.

We are also working in homes for abandoned, handicapped children who also suffer from Parkinson's Disease and Down's Syndrome. The Government provides only 80 cents a day for food and medicine for the whole of a children's home! Half of them can't even get off their beds they are so exhausted.

Life in Russia since the end of Communism has been worse, and eighty per cent of the population are now living below the poverty line. Industry has collapsed. Many systems such as Education, Health and Science have been destroyed and industry is non-existent. In World War II, during the hardest times ever experienced, when the enemy was close to Moscow, we lost only twenty-four per cent of our industry. Since 1991, almost all of our industry has been destroyed.

Conditions continue to worsen for people and the Government has already planned further cuts in welfare of fifteen per cent. The future for the people is very difficult and I personally believe that Russia is experiencing the judgement of the Lord for the past years of ungodliness that began in 1917. We come to the Lord much more easily when we are in a tough situation and that is exactly what is happening. There is great revival because the crisis has reminded us of the need for God, and that only he is faithful and only he can show the way. Russia must repent immediately to receive God's forgiveness. Russia *needs* God's love now!

I am so happy and blessed because I've met the Lord God. Of course, he had to teach me a hard lesson through the helicopter crash. It was very hard, but our Heavenly Father is a real father and he *knew* that it needed something dramatic. I know that if this had not happened to me, no one would ever have convinced me of the existence of the Lord God. Never!

When people ask me, 'How did you survive the crash?' I tell them, 'God saved me' and they believe me! My wife, my two daughters, my sons-in-law and all my relatives became Christians because they could see that only the Lord God could have saved me. Jesus means everything to me. Every day of my life that I live, is a new day from him. I don't know what tomorrow will bring, but I must live *this day* not for myself, but for his glory

Half of them can't even get off their beds

From the book *Operation World*

The spectacular demise of Communism took the world by surprise. Open Doors and others called for a **seven-year campaign of prayer for the Soviet Union in 1984*** with the specific goal of complete religious liberty and Bibles available for all. **This was achieved in 1990/91**! Praise God!**

Author's note

(Helicopter crash 1984! Evangelist allowed on General Borisov's Base 1991!)

REYNARD FABER

My grandfather, who was the last traditional chief of the Apaches, passed away in 1964 when I was around two years old. Knowing he was dying, he called his family together and told them, 'You need to go down a spiritual path and start attending church in order for the family to stay together and have a right way of life.' But sadly, the family didn't do that. Many of them died from alcoholism and I even found one of my relatives frozen in the snow one winter.

I was born on Christmas Day in Santa Fe, New Mexico at the Indian hospital. We lived in a one-roomed log cabin that had a dirt floor, no running water, and just a kerosene lamp for light. My father and mother had an arranged marriage that didn't last very long because of his alcohol problem. Once when I was little my father came home drunk, fought with my mother, and pushed her into my high chair. I fell on top of the stove she was cooking on, and still have the scars on my hands. My father was drunk all the time, and eventually he abandoned us.

Mom was a nurse and when she was working, we stayed with my grandma. She's the one who really raised us and taught us our Apache ways. We were brought up very traditionally and spoke no English, just Apache. We were like hillbillies! We used to hitch up the horses and wagon and go with my uncle into town to buy our groceries.

Around noon or early afternoon the Apache women would spread out their blankets on the ground. They'd take some lunch meat, melons, cookies and soda pops that they had bought at the trading post and we would all get together and have a good picnic. Someone would watch the ground and the shadows, and they'd know when it was time to go home before it got dark.

Prior to going to school, when I was about four and a half or five years old, I had a really bad accident. I was standing on the porch playing with my cousins and the next thing I knew I was lying on the ground. I had fallen off the porch somehow and hit my head and neck on a rock. I couldn't move. I was there for perhaps ten or fifteen minutes and all I could do was look at the clouds drifting by. I couldn't even shout.

I was put into an ambulance, one of the old, bubble-shaped types. I could move nothing but my eyes. We drove fast and I could see the mountains outside flashing by. During the journey to Santa Fe I went into a coma and was put onto a respirator.

According to my mother, they visited me every day but I couldn't waken up. The doctors were trying to decide on whether to operate or unplug the respirator. My mother's cousin told her not to let them cut my skull open, or I would become like a vegetable. She and mom discussed what to do and felt that if I didn't respond when they unplugged the machine — that was that. Mom told the doctors to unplug it, and when they did one by one all my functions ceased. For about ten minutes I was 'dead'. I wasn't breathing; my heart wasn't pumping. Then I 'woke up', still paralysed, but I found I could blink my eyes.

I remained in the hospital for many months doing various kinds of therapy. There were little rails on the wall, which I hung onto and practised walking. I had to identify different coloured wood blocks, etc. When it came time for me to go home my legs weren't sufficiently strong, so they recommended that I rode a tricycle, which they gave me. It was a metallic burgundy colour with big wheels covered in stars and little streamers on the handlebars! I used to ride it around the house at my grandma's.

> **I wasn't breathing; my heart wasn't pumping**

REYNARD FABER

My accident and recovery caused great difficulties for me. Before that time, I was the favourite child out of my brothers and cousins because I had been born on Christmas Day. When I returned from the hospital, it was very different. Since the doctors said I had died in hospital and come back to life, they were afraid of me. The Apaches are very superstitious about death so they avoided me and were unkind. I spent a lot of my childhood alone, herding sheep.

In the early 1800s the Government had a strategy to eradicate the Indians — total genocide. When that didn't work, they decided to assimilate them, so they put them on Reservations. Part of the process was to send missionaries to the Reservations to 'Christianise'. They did this, not by sharing spiritual things, but by trying to change our whole outlook, a total makeover. They cut off our hair, threw our buckskin clothes away, gave us white man's clothes, and punished us severely for speaking Apache instead of English. By the time I went to school, the Government had left schooling to the missionaries.

When I was six years old, government officials told my mom and grandma that all children over the age of six had to be enrolled in the boarding school they had built on our Reservation. My mom told them that we were able to provide schooling ourselves, but they said that was no good. Even though I was only six I can remember them saying, 'If you don't send your child to the boarding school today, we will take him and you will be put in prison for six months.' Mom didn't want to go to prison. Either way she was going to lose me so she packed my clothes in brown paper bags and the Government people took me to the boarding school.

I tried to escape but he caught me . . .

As soon as I arrived, they started mistreating me; I was crying and was uncooperative I suppose. They took off all my clothes put me in a shower room with lots of other kids my age and turned on the hot water. I had never seen a shower; we were still drawing water from outside to take a bath! The matrons had great long sticks and if they saw someone not under the shower, they would hit them. Anyone whose hair didn't squeak when they came out was sent back in again. Some of my friends and I huddled in the corner scared stiff! I was in that boarding school from the age of six through to eleven years old.

My mother, who had by then remarried, came to take my brothers and I away from the boarding school. My stepfather was from Oklahoma so we moved there. This was my first time away from the Reservation. He was a nasty man and got drunk and fought with my mom all the time, beating her until there was blood on the walls. He then started fighting with my brothers and me.

The first time he beat me, he kicked me all over, arms, legs, face and stomach. I was only eleven and a puny child; I tried to escape but he caught me and continued with the beating. I lost consciousness and when I came to, I was alone; my mom and my stepfather had gone. I couldn't walk or get up so I crawled into the room where I slept on the floor. The next morning the pillow had dried on my face. I peeled it off, crawled into the washroom to get a cold washing rag, and started wiping my face. When I saw myself in the mirror, I was really afraid and didn't go to school for the rest of the year.

I was beaten up again and this time I ran over to the neighbours' house to try to call the police, but they didn't want to call. My stepfather stormed into their house without knocking, holding a sawn-off shotgun, and grabbed me by the collar of my shirt, opened the door and dragged me out. He said that if I ever tried to call the police again, he would shoot me. He pointed the gun right into my face!

The third time he beat me, I ran to the same neighbours' house. He came after me again, but this time they wouldn't let him in and they called the police, who came and took him away. As a result my brothers and I were then sent to another boarding school in Oklahoma. I became withdrawn and wouldn't talk to anybody. I hated everybody!

At around this time I met Ray Tracey. He was a movie star who had just made a new film. He was a Native American who visited our school and took Assembly. I had been awarded good merit points for cleaning my room and other such things so I was allowed to go the movie premier with him. Before he left he said to me, 'Don't let what has happened to you stop you from achieving what you want to do in life. Start talking and start *doing* things. Whoever did this to you is no longer here, so you can start again. I want you to start living *tomorrow* and join in the school activities.'

The following day I was like a different person. I began talking to my roommates and we became good friends. I joined a wrestling team and a swimming team at the YMCA and started selling concessions with my class at the football games. I stood for the position of First Officer of the Student Body at Mid High and only lost by one point. Eventually I told them I wanted to move back home to the Reservation. I wanted to stay with my grandma, but they wouldn't let me, so I ended up back in my old boarding school on the Reservation.

I discovered that all the kids had become really bad; they were always getting into trouble, and swore all the time. I was considered the 'new' kid, and got into lots of fistfights. It wasn't until I was in 10th grade in boarding school that I decided I wasn't going to let anybody push me around any more. I was lanky and skinny, but I could get quite nasty.

In order to survive, if anybody looked at me in the wrong way, or if they whispered something behind my back, I would hit them or kick them. I was going to drop out in 10th grade, but the Student Council Sponsor encouraged me to stay on and finish school. I said, 'What for?' He said if I stood for Student Council, he wouldn't bother me any more and I could drop out if I wanted. But if I won, I had to finish school. I agreed, because I knew I wasn't going to win. I ran against a Senior and I ended up becoming the Student Body President! I became active at school, playing basketball and running track events.

I was the first one in my family to graduate from High School, and not one of them showed up, they were all drunk; that was the biggest disappointment of my whole life. All those years I had *tried* to be good in spite of being ostracised since returning from hospital, beaten up by my stepfather, going through readjustment at the Reservation due to being the 'new' kid, and I had felt my parents would reward me by coming. I didn't want presents or anything like that. I just wanted them to *be* there. There were only seventeen in my graduation class and at the receiving line; none of my family was there. I was *really* angry and upset.

Someone came up to me and said, 'As you didn't get any presents, here's a bottle of champagne!' not knowing that I'd just decided to get permanently drunk! For the next two years I got drunk every day. I was always looking for something to drink, and people with whom to drink it. I became one of the town's habitual drunks. Some days I would wake up in a ditch, covered in mud, my hair, clothes, everything, hung over, vomiting and would then get drunk again. I didn't care.

One day I was sitting outside the shopping centre at the Reservation waiting for the bar to open. I was 19 years old. I had been out all Sunday night, drinking, and I was a mess! My grandma's cousin was working behind the counter, selling the dry goods. I asked her for some money to buy juice because I had a hangover. She searched in her purse but said, 'Before I give it to you, I want to say this to you. *Don't drink any more*. It's just false happiness. I'm praying for you.'

I didn't pay any attention because she'd said such things to me before. She'd tried to encourage me to go to College, to do something good with my life, not to waste it. I bought the apple juice and sat down outside with some other drunks.

I just wanted them to *be* there

As I waited for the bar to open at 9 o'clock in the morning her words kept pounding in my mind, 'Don't drink any more. It's just false happiness. I'm praying for you.' I closed my eyes trying block out her words. When I opened my eyes, I was *completely sober*.

It was like waking up. I looked around and I could see myself clearly. I was a mess. I saw the awful reality of what I was doing to myself, and I saw my drinking companions clearly. They were drunk, hung-over, laughing, waiting for the bar to open. I got up and I said, 'I'm not going to drink any more from this day on.' I had been drinking with them for two years. They laughed and said, 'We'll see you back here tomorrow!' 'No,' I said, 'you won't.'

I walked down to my grandma's house and slept. When I awoke she had a bath ready for me, a big metal washtub filled with hot water from those old kettles on the stove. She said, 'You'd better take a bath.' That was all! So I did. My face was a mess, covered in cysts, acne, cuts, etc, and Grandma found some Indian medicine that she'd pounded from the roots. She told me to wash my face with that for several weeks. I did so, and it cleared up.

During that time, emptiness began to grow in me. I became anxious because there was something that I needed but didn't know what. I walked up through the canyon and into the forest where I lay down on a rock and watch the bears pass by. I watched the eagles circling in the sky and saw the hawks dive down to catch their prey; I walked along the trails and watched the deer; I walked along the creek and remembered how, when we were little, we used to catch the fish with our hands and then let them go. Being in the forest was so peaceful. Every day I went to experience its peace and began casting my mind back to when we were doing ceremonies in the forest. I had felt at peace then.

I rolled it up and was about to throw it in the stove . . .

I decided to become a medicine man, in order to get this peace. There were some good things but because there were questionable things, like putting curses on people, I did not complete the training. One night, with many unanswered questions and frustration, I went for a walk in the hills. On the way down I came to a halt feeling particularly angry and said, 'God, how come you made the stars in the sky, the deer in the forest, the grass of the fields and the fish in the brooks, but you can't help *me*?' I went home in tears, to bed.

The next day my grandma woke me saying, 'We're going to clean today, so I need your help.' She pointed at a blue dresser in the back room of our old house, 'There's a lot of junk in there. Throw it out, and burn the paper in the wood stove.' There were old magazines and comic books and I was burning it all when I came across part of a book with very thin pages. I rolled it up and was about to throw it in the stove when I decided to have a look at it and saw the word GOD. This book had no cover on it; many of the pages were gone; others were torn out, soiled, stuck together. It was very thin. But I kept it.

I read stories in this ragged old book about people meeting a man called Jesus, and everywhere he went, somebody's life was changed.

I read about a woman at a well, and how he met her and talked to her, asked her about her personal life and her previous husbands, and when she said, 'I have no husband,' he replied, 'You are right … the man you now have is not your husband.' She was so amazed that she went to her village and said to them 'Come, see a man who told me everything I ever did. Could this be the Christ?' Because of the woman's testimony, many believed.

I then read the story about the woman caught in adultery and how the Pharisees wanted to stone her but when they brought her to Jesus he said, 'If anyone one of you is without sin, let him be the first to throw a stone at her.' And they couldn't. It says that he knelt down on the ground again and wrote something. When he got up he said, 'Woman, where are they? Has no-one condemned you?' And she said, 'No-one, sir.' He replied, 'Neither do I condemn you.

Go now and leave your life of sin.' There was another story about ten lepers who were cleansed from leprosy and were healed, and one turned around and said thank you, and Jesus replied, 'Your faith has made you well.'

I was so amazed at all these stories that I said, 'God, I wish there was a real Jesus who could come and change my life.' Then I read about Bartimaeus on the road to Jericho and how Jesus gave him his sight back. I read about the demonic in Mark Chapter 5, the man with so many unclean spirits. In verse 7 it says that the man came running and fell at Jesus' feet, and the evil spirits called him the Son of the Most High God. I knew then that Jesus was real and that he was the Son of the Most High God. He commanded all those unclean spirits to come out of the man, and they obeyed, and went into a herd of pigs and were drowned in the lake. It said that the man was found, sitting clothed and in his right mind at the feet of Jesus. At the very beginning, this man was naked, lived in the graveyard and cut himself with rocks. No-one could tame him, and the people were afraid. Now, here he was, sitting that same day, that same hour, clothed, in his right mind, at the feet of Jesus! I felt, 'Wow! That's power!'

I turned another page, and I was in John Chapter 3, reading a story about a religious man, Nicodemus, to whom Jesus said he had to be born again. And I had the same question as Nicodemus: 'How can I be born again when I'm already grown up?' I kept on reading and realised that *I* needed to be born again, and that Jesus could give me a changed life.

I fell on the ground, because God came to me. There was a presence there. I didn't see anything, but somebody was talking to me from the words in the book and I felt a very strong presence — not fearful — but there. And I began to weep, because when this presence came into the room and when I heard somebody speak to me using the words from the book, it showed me *who I really was*. I said, 'God, I can't come to you. My life is full of filth, trash, and guilt. Why do you want me?'

I told God all the bad things I'd ever done, as if he didn't know! It was like one of those days when I had my worst hangover, when I was all muddy, *but even more so*. And I said, 'Why do you want me? I can't come to you like this, the way I am.' I picked up the book again, and read John 3:16–18 and it was as if somebody was speaking these words to me, 'For God so loved the world, that he gave his one and only Son that *whoever* believes in him shall not perish, but have eternal life.' And it continued, 'For God did not send his Son into the world to condemn the world, but to save the world through him. Whoever believes in him is not condemned, but whoever does not believe stands condemned already because he has not believed in the name of God's one and only Son.' I knew I had to make a decision that day if I wanted a changed life, and I knew that I couldn't help myself.

I was carrying a lot of hurt from the past. I told God about that. I didn't make any deal with him! I just said, 'If you'll give me a changed life, forgive me for all the bad things I've ever done, come into my life and change me, *I'll go anywhere you want me to go, I'll do anything you want me to do and say anything you want me to say. Just give me a changed life.'* It was so weird because it seemed that the presence that was in that room came inside me. I was the happiest person in the whole world. I was so excited.

I picked up the book, and read the first verse I saw: 'If anyone is in Christ, he is a new creation: the old has gone, the new has come!' And I *knew* I was new. I felt *brand spanking new*.

Immediately after I was saved and Jesus changed my life I prayed, 'I want a job, Lord, and get me off the Reservation. Move me somewhere.' That same week I moved to Colorado and got a job at a Christian hostel and book store, called The Gospel House, which had been started by some Christian businessmen in the community. I had no place to live, knew nobody there, but had my job arranged.

> **It was so weird because it seemed that the presence . . .**

REYNARD FABER

When I arrived I saw a man making beef stew. I said, 'Excuse me, I need a place to stay for a couple of days. Can I stay here?' And he replied, 'This is the Lord's house. Stay as long as you want.' And I said, 'Say that again!?' He repeated, 'This is the Lord's house. You can stay as long as you want. I'm having supper soon, you can join me.' I was so happy; I stayed there for six months.

Every Thursday they had a Bible Study, Praise and Worship. It was so new to me. The only time anyone in my family said they loved me was when they were drunk! So the first time somebody else told me that, I was so embarrassed. They were sober, and it was a man! He was teaching in the Fellowship about God's love and said, 'Rey, if you see me down the street when I'm driving by in my pickup, and you're trying to wave at me and get my attention, if for some reason I don't see you I want you to be assured that I love you. You don't ever have to doubt that.' And that is how God's love was explained to me.

I was discipled, baptised, and six months later moved back to the Reservation. I was on an emotional seesaw because I had no church, no Christian friends, and I felt depressed. One of my cousins said, 'I know you're depressed, but if you say that you believe in God the way that you do, you'd better snap out of it. You go home, you get on your knees and you pray and ask God to give you strength. Tomorrow you'll start living for God again.' He dropped me off. I went inside, got down on my knees and prayed, 'God I can't live this Christian life in my own strength. I need your help all the time.' The next morning I felt brand new again. That cousin who took me home is still not a believer, but God really used him at that time.

Shortly after that, while working for the newspaper, writing stories and articles, and giving my testimony in the paper, one of my assignments was to interview a missionary family who were holding meetings in a trailer home in the middle of a mud field. I discovered they were going to build a church and said I would help, so I joined and became the first member. Within six months, we had ninety people coming from the Reservation. I knew that God was calling me to the ministry full time and I surrendered to this in April 1985.

I attended Bible school at Liberty University in Virginia. The tribe that I'm from had promised to pay for my schooling, but when I arrived, there was no money. They said they would not pay because it was a religious school. So there I was, in Virginia, with no money to pay for my schooling but I went ahead anyway, and registered for all my classes. When it came time to settle my finances, I told them that I had no money at all so they sent me to talk to a Financial Aid Counsellor. He asked why I was attending school there. I told him I was an Apache Indian and that I was attending school there because God had called me to take the gospel to the Indians when I finished my schooling. He told me to wait and went away for ten minutes. When he returned, he told me I was in! I did not have to pay anything! I found school hard, but I made it through by God's grace.

After graduation, I went home to the Reservation and worked as assistant Director for the Tribal Youth Programmes. For three years, I worked with between 500 and 700 kids on a daily basis, and then went back to the seminary in Virginia as a graduate assistant.

In the summer of 1995 I had been on a missions tour which involved travelling in a van for two weeks. I thought I would get some books from the library. I had always heard about Billy Graham but I didn't really know who he was. So I took out four books about him and, as I read one of them telling about how God had used him, it really touched my heart. I had the book over my face because I didn't want the people in the library to see me crying. And I prayed, 'God, if you would just give me a small part of this man's ministry, it would be the desire of my heart,' but I didn't really expect the Lord to do anything about it!

> **I was so embarrassed. They were sober, and it was a man!**

Various ministries I was due to be involved with during the Summer were cancelled, as well as some in the Fall. I said, 'God, what are you doing? What do you have in store for me? I know it's something better than what I had organised.' The phone rang. It was a Crusade director for Billy Graham Ministries! He said Franklin Graham was holding a Crusade in New Mexico and they wanted me at the meetings! They ended up hiring me to liaise with the churches for the Crusade.

Two-thirds of the people who attended the Crusade every night were Native American and many were saved. There's still a lot of follow-up being done. During the Crusade, Franklin introduced me to Pastor Skip Heitzig from Calvary Chapel. When it was finished he said he wanted me to go to Albuquerque to help Skip. There I started doing Native American outreach.

During the late- or mid-1500s the church persecuted the Native Americans, and forced them to join, threatening them with death. Some were made examples of, and then they were enslaved. In 1680 all the Indians got together, the Apaches, the Navahos, the Pueblos and the Comanches and chased out the Europeans, burning down their churches. It is very hard work, but with God's grace and help, we are able to get in. The leaders have become more receptive to us because we were helping their people. I will continue to do this work until God leads me somewhere else. I can do lots of things that I'm good at, but if God doesn't want me there, I have no business doing them. *I have to be where he wants me to be, not where Reynard wants to be.*

My family is now saved and my stepfather (the one who used to beat me) and I have the best possible relationship. God has healed me and he has healed my family. Every Christian needs to work through those issues in their own lives. I was a Christian for almost eight years and I never dealt with that. One day visiting my Mom's house I saw my stepfather there. I had always felt angry and wanted to kick him. As a Christian I knew it was wrong to think that, but I felt it more and more. I talked to a pastor who suggested I see a Christian counsellor. When I told him the whole story he said, 'You need to let it go. You need to cut the shackles and stop dragging it around with you.' And that is what I did. I closed my eyes and prayed that God would set me free. I cut the shackles and forgave him and I haven't had those bitter or resentful feelings towards him ever since. We have a good relationship because God came into our family and changed it.

My life is fulfilled, even though I do mess things up once in a while. In 1 Corinthians Chapter 13 it says, 'Love is patient.' That's how I see God, patient with me and patient with the whole human race. It is difficult to comprehend because we are so impatient in this 'instant' world. We want people to change right away. We want new converts to become super Christians by next week! But it's a process I'm still going through.

Jesus has said that he will never leave us nor forsake us and just because we go through hardships, that doesn't mean that he has abandoned us. He's there with us and as we focus on him and trust him through it all, we become more like him. Being a Christian for me isn't living a 'religious' life but it is living in a personal relationship with my creator.

Cut the shackles and stop

Finally one man said, 'Tiger'!

My grandfather was a head-hunter. In fact, he was not only a head-hunter but he was head cutter! In a football team, not all eleven players are goal scorers, only two or three are strikers. My grandfather, Odanghetea was one of those head cutters. I still don't know whether I'm proud or ashamed to be his grandson.

In the late 1800s Dr E. W. Clark, a pioneer Baptist missionary to India, went from village to village telling people about Jesus Christ. He and some converts came to my ancestral village of Changki and preached in the square. People gathered there to listen to this white man talk about a new God called Jesus Christ. They heard about a religion full of love, forgiveness and reconciliation, and that if you believed in him you would go to heaven. This was the simple gospel message they gave.

Later Dr Clark brought a long bamboo pole and placed it across the village square saying, 'Those of you who would like to become followers of Jesus Christ and accept this new religion, cross over.' Our people were primitive and backward, we were animists who worshipped spirits, stones, wood, trees, rivers and mountains. There was much superstition and reluctance that day but some people crossed over the bamboo saying, 'Whatever happens, I will become a follower of Jesus.' Among them was my grandfather and that's how I inherited the Christian faith.

I am the eldest of twelve children, born in 1920. My father was a teacher in a mission school and my mother, like most others in those days, was illiterate. We lived in a thatched house in the middle of what we called the mission compound. It was between two large villages and surrounded by jungle where there were tigers, wolves, bears and other wild animals. My father looked after cows and pigs and would sell them to supplement his low salary. Occasionally, the tigers would come and take them away and that was scary!

One morning as my brother Amos and I came up from the spring with two pails of water, about halfway home we saw some people with spears and long knives running towards the jungle. I asked one of them, 'Where are you going?' Nobody bothered to answer because we were kids, but finally one man said, 'Tiger'! I turned to Amos, 'They are going on a tiger hunt. Shall we go?' He didn't say anything but seemed to agree, so we left the pails by the side of the road and rushed into the jungle.

That day they killed five tigers. That was our first experience of seeing tigers being speared to death by the village people and it was exciting. This happened about 1928–29. By the time we got home it was dark and we were very hungry because we had gone all day without food and water. We found that the door was locked on the inside so we shouted, 'Daddy, Mummy, open the door. We have killed five tigers!' Nobody answered. We shouted again, 'Daddy, Mummy, open the door, we are hungry.' Not a word. Finally my father said, 'You sleep with the five dead tigers tonight! Where are the buckets of water we sent you for in the morning? Who gave you permission to go into the jungle?' Amos and I both started crying so loudly that my mother finally opened the door and gave us food. Soon afterwards my father brought a cane and beat us because of what we had done. That day we learned discipline.

As the eldest in the family, and because it was a long time before I had sisters, I was responsible for many of the chores around the home. I had to miss playing football and volleyball but the discipline of the work helped me to be good in my studies. Almost every year I came out top in my class.

DR IMCHABA BENDANG WATI

To my great surprise scores of people would stand up

I became a college graduate with the help of Dr John William Cook, a missionary from the USA, who came to my rescue. I was about to drop out of college because I had no financial support when he said that he and the memsahib, his wife, would like to support me. Very happily I continued with my studies. For the next two years he kept asking me, 'Ben Wati, would you like to go to America for Bible studies?' I said that I wasn't interested in either Bible studies or in going to the USA as I wanted to become a lawyer or get an MA in India.

As my college education drew to an end, many things happened. Mr Ghandi had his National Movement against the British Raj, saying 'Quit India.' There was a tremendous national movement especially among the youth and I was one of them. Then came the Great Bengal famine of Calcutta in which many died on the streets. During World War II I was studying at St Paul's College in Calcutta because all the colleges of North East India were closed, and there I met my future wife, Nirmala. She used to play the piano on Sunday evenings when a few of us got together for singing and prayer.

I became restless regarding my future so one day I prayed, 'God, help me come to a decision on whether or not I should go to America.' The next morning I said to the college Principal, 'Sir, there's a suggestion that I go to America for Bible studies. What do you say?' He replied, 'If there is an opportunity, I would go, because the church in India needs an educated ministry.' So in December 1943 I wrote to Dr Cook and said, 'I'm willing to work with you and then go to America.' I graduated from Calcutta University with a BA in 1944 and then assisted Dr Cook in teaching at a Christian High School for one year. In July 1945, soon after VE day, I was among 3,000 passengers on a Swedish ship going to the States. I studied for my BD at the Northern Baptist Seminary in Chicago and then in 1949 received my MA at Wheaton College.

One of the things I have learned in my life is to read the Scriptures. When I was a student at Wheaton College, I heard a Chinese evangelist say that he read five Psalms and one chapter of Proverbs every day. He finished both books once a month. The Book of Psalms teaches me how to relate to God, how to worship him, how to pray to him, how to praise him and how to thank him. The Book of Proverbs enables me to relate to man in the world, how to be vigilant, how to avoid temptations and how to be wise. I have tried to emulate this as far as possible.

After finishing my studies in the USA, I returned to India where I married Nirmala in October 1950, and worked as a lecturer at the Jorhat Bible College that I had helped to found. I enjoyed teaching and God blessed me but he took me out of the classroom. In 1952 I was asked to join the Evangelical Fellowship of India who worked for the revival of the church.

After praying with Nirmala for several months, I accepted and became involved not only on the national scene, but internationally as well. On the journey back to India from the USA, I had started to pray, 'Help me to be a blessing to one person every day.' There were times when nothing much happened but I found when I spoke at a meeting, a conference, or convention, to my great surprise scores of people would stand up and respond to my simple message to become Christians. In 1966 I was involved with the First World Congress on Evangelism, which was held in Berlin, and in 1974 at the Congress in Lausanne. Following that I became a member of the continuing committee with Dr Billy Graham.

In 1968 I was elected President of the World Evangelical Fellowship, which I felt I did not deserve; yet God took me there. I have been a missionary at large in North-east India for many years and held positions in different organisations but perhaps one of the best things I did for my people was to help translate the Bible into my own Ao Naga language. The first Naga Bible was published in 1964. I have tried to serve the Lord to the best of my ability, and by God's grace, I have seen fruits for my labour. I want everything to be for his glory.

As I look back over the last 125 years of Christianity brought to us by the Baptist missionaries, it is beyond understanding how God has been so gracious to our people. There has been so much blessing in Nagaland and ninety percent of our people are now Christians. Recently I was able to preach to 2,200 in one church on Palm Sunday and then 3,200 in another church on Easter Sunday. The people arrive at church one hour before the services start in order to get a seat because so many people attend. There is a tremendous interest in spite of the fact that there is insurgency among our people. Underground factions fight one another with much bloodshed and the church is suffering. But, in spite of all that, the Spirit of God is working and I am quite encouraged.

I believe that the Lord has been guiding and directing my life. When I was about nine or ten years old, I can remember one day sitting under the shade of an old oak tree near our house. I was thinking about what I would like to become or do, and asked myself, 'If there was only one wish in all the world what would I choose?'

After thinking for a long time, I said 'I would like to go to heaven.' Of course, I did not know then that it is impossible to go to heaven just by merely wishing, but later on when I was fourteen years old, I came to know Jesus Christ and was assured of my salvation through reading a New Testament given to me by my father. Now I am certain that I'll go to heaven.

I then wondered what would I choose if I had a second wish. After a while I said, 'I would like to go once around the world.' My geography teacher had told us that the earth was round like an orange and if we started from Impur where I was born, and went up and down the hills, across the rivers and oceans, we would come straight back home. I could hardly believe it but I wanted to try. I wanted to venture out and go around the world.

Once more I said to myself, 'If I had a third wish, what would I do, what would I choose? Should I become a rich man, should I become a doctor, should I become an Army Captain?' All sorts of things came to my mind and finally I said, 'If I had a third choice, I would like to be healthy and not sick like some of the others in the village.'

Those were the three choices I made in my childhood. I thank God that it was like a vision and I can testify that when I die, I shall go to heaven; secondly because God is able to give abundantly more than we ask or even think, I went around the world at least twice by ship and several times by plane. I thank God for the privilege, and praise him that for the last eighty-two years I can confidently say that I have been sick only eighty-two days. That is one day for each year. Of course, I realise that some time or another I may suddenly have a dreadful disease that will take me home to the Lord but . . . so far so good.

> **I did not know then that it is impossible to go to heaven . . .**

I was born into a Hindu family where my parents taught me to worship idols. We had a little temple in our house before which we were sent to bow our head every morning and every evening.

When I was about seven years old we had a lot of family problems. I saw my parents fighting and was quite alarmed at the degree of violence that I witnessed. My younger brother and I didn't understand what was really going on, but another man began to come to our house and I had a hunch that he was the cause of all the troubles.

Changes happened rapidly after that and one day my father walked out. He just walked out! His parents lived close by so he went there because where else could he go? My brother began to cry so much that my mother packed a little bundle for him and told a servant to drop him where my father's parents lived. That was the last I saw of him as a family — that day our family broke up completely.

Presumably wanting to escape from all the mess, my mother took me out of school and moved us from Bombay to Delhi. Because she wanted to work and look after herself there was no choice but to put me in a hostel at a boarding school. Those early years were very traumatic — as a result of all that had happened my father became sick and died. Everyone told me he loved my mother to the last day. I had a wonderful relationship with my father and really loved him so I resented my mother for many years.

Consequently I was insecure and searching for something. I began to hear about God when I was only eleven and at about sixteen years of age something momentous happened. Sheila came to our school to talk about Jesus. She invited me to a Youth for Christ Camp — actually it was a discipleship camp, not really for unbelievers at all, but I was very keen to go.

When I arrived, I saw such happy faces. The young people were really worshipping the Lord and I knew they had something that I didn't have. I was completely caught up by the atmosphere — I could sense that God was present there, and I knew that whatever it was, was real.

They seemed to have an inner joy, and they would say such wonderful things about this Jesus, about whom I hardly knew anything. I was never given a Bible, I didn't know who Jesus was, what he taught or did. I actually had no idea at all. But what they said about Jesus was so different from what I had heard about the various gods who seemed dead and had no life to them. This person Jesus really seemed to be alive!

On the last day of the camp I said this short prayer all by myself; nobody invited me to an altar call — nothing — I just prayed, 'If all this is real and all this is true then I really want you to come into my life and I want to follow you and I want to have the same joy that everybody else has.' At the end of it, I felt so light, as if I was floating. It was mixed with a joy that just came into my being and after a lovely sleep that night I woke up in the morning feeling wonderful. I was so happy that I told everybody that I really felt Jesus had come into my life.

They gave me a Bible and I found that I was able to understand what was written in it. All the verses were clear to me and I began to devour it. I loved every word and I wouldn't put it down. When I went back to the hostel everybody said, 'Your face looks so radiant; you look so full of happiness, what happened to you?' I shared the whole experience with them and within just a few days some of my friends came to know the Lord.

> # That was the last I saw of him . . .

It'll be stinking, filthy and hot!

After leaving boarding school the following year I went to university where I had a wonderful opportunity to go to an evangelistic church; my faith grew a lot as I worshipped there. My entire life was transformed and there was no comparison between the 'before' and the 'after'. I realised how miserable I had been in the past because of my family so I said to the Lord, 'My life doesn't belong to me. It just belongs to you. I had no life before you and now I'll do whatever you say. Anything that you ask me to do, I will do.'

I felt very drawn to medicine and started with the pre-medical course at university. In India things are very difficult. There are between 10,000 and 15,000 candidates for just 300 seats in the University of Delhi. So I prayed, 'Lord, I don't know what you want me to become — if it's a doctor then I suppose it doesn't matter whether there are 15,000 or 15 million, that seat will be there for me.' I gave everything into God's hands, and I got into a very good medical college. I really enjoyed my studies, did very well, and before I knew it, I had completed the course.

When training in the hospital, my heart went out to the poor people because they came with all sorts of sicknesses and had no money. Sometimes we didn't have enough medicine and felt so helpless. A well of compassion for these people grew within me. I really wanted to help, and more and more the Lord confirmed that this is what I would do.

In 1985 I finished my postgraduate studies in Paediatrics. Most people in my group either went abroad to the UK or the US. Government jobs were also very popular — people pursued them because they offered job security, a pension and many other benefits — but I knew that was not what God wanted me to do.

After three years working with an organisation called Sharan, I felt God saying to me that this was the time and I was ready to start something new. I said to him, 'Lord, I know you're sending me to the poorest of the poor.' I had worked in the middle of a resettlement colony and the conditions were bad but I knew there were people in much worse conditions and that's where I really wanted to be.

My friends were concerned. 'We don't know whether you'll be able to handle it because the slums are so dirty — there's no water supply, no sanitation, no building — it'll be stinking, filthy and hot! There will be flies and mosquitoes, everything, human beings all in one little patch of land, one on top of another because there are so many of them.' I replied, 'If Jesus were walking here today then I am very sure that is exactly where we would find him. I want to walk in his steps and I'll go to the worst colonies to help the people.'

I felt very inadequate because I'd never been in such a dirty situation before but I felt God's presence and I knew that he was going before me. The day I made the decision to start ASHA in August 1988, my whole being was at peace because I knew this was right. There was a cholera epidemic in the city at that time and so many people were dying in the slums, especially little children, mostly because they didn't have good clean drinking water.

The hospitals were flooded with children. Every bed had five, six or even seven of them lying with drips hanging from everywhere. This is the situation I went into. I hadn't planned to start in August, I thought I would go around first and just look, but the situation was so compelling I couldn't go away from it. The slum people were begging me, 'This is the time we desperately need you.' So, with nothing except a suitcase full of medicines, physician samples etc, I used to jump the fence into the slum.

It was very dense inside with crowded little huts made out of mud and brick with plastic sheeting on top. The slum leader gave me a little place outside his hut and I saw lines of patients from morning until evening. I bought red paint and together with some other community members I painted all the unsafe hand pumps and told the people, 'Don't drink water from the ones painted red.' Many lives were saved and that gave me an instant relationship with them.

Throughout the crisis I found myself thinking 'How can I ignore this type of poverty?' In the beginning I ran my clinic, then in the evening they sat down and told me about how there were no drains, no toilets and the women had no place to go. There was no dignity for them as human beings they had to perform their toilet in front of everybody — such a shameful situation.

I had lived in the city for many years and I only understood their condition when I actually went right inside to work among them. I felt compelled to help them in all these different ways and realised that giving them medicines was not going to solve the problem. If I really wanted the health status of this whole population to improve, then I must help them to get clean water and proper drains. They dug holes outside their little huts with some crude instrument and whatever dirty water came out of their homes collected in that hole. It took about three days for the hole to fill and then they would throw it out. That was the only drainage arrangement they made and as the hole was not covered you can imagine the flies with all that dirty smelly water.

Somehow the Lord gave me such a love for them that I didn't mind the stink or the environment; I never felt, 'Oh, I shouldn't touch this.' I ate and drank with them while sitting on the dirty floors of their little huts and prayed 'Keep me in good health.' Every condition that is conducive to tuberculosis was there with seven or eight people living in a tiny little hut of maybe 15 sq. ft. People said that every second house had TB, and I would get TB or diarrhoea or some other illness, that it was too risky for me and for my family! I'd reply, 'God has called me. God will protect me.' And he has. In all these years I have never fallen sick, not even once.

I became very popular with the people because I used to sit down and listen to their problems. The local politicians are supposed to solve the problems but these places were so dirty, that no politician wanted to enter. They only came around for five minutes when they wanted votes.

Within four or five months of my being there the Government came in to do some work and noticed me. They became interested in what I was doing and we began to collaborate on many different things. I said, 'You must help them with drainage and sanitation because there is no point in my running a health care system here without that.' They were very supportive and suddenly there were water points, there was a drain, there was a road; all these things happened within about six months and it was unrecognisable as the same colony.

As word got around, I was flooded with requests from the other slums in the area to come and help them. I also started receiving requests from the Government, which was very unusual. They don't normally like to work with volunteer organisations and are always suspicious but when they saw me in that environment they were immediately convinced of my sincerity. From the beginning they wanted me to open more clinics. The slum commissioner said, 'I won't leave you alone until you open at least fifteen clinics.' I said I had never even dreamt of the number — I was thinking about one or two colonies at the most. I am only one human being, so how much can I do? But he said, 'We have a scheme whereby we can provide you with a proper building and you don't have to worry about funds for that, you just ask your donors to give you money for running the whole show.'

Within three years we had opened fifteen clinics. It was one of those amazing periods, definitely supernatural, because humanly speaking such things are virtually impossible. Transformations in even one or two slums may take a lifetime, but God seemed to be doing it. His heart was so full of love for these people and he desperately wanted to reach out to them.

I don't know why he decided to choose me for this work but I made myself available to him and said, 'Lord, I am full of energy. I'm young. I still have many years ahead of me and have nothing else to do except serve you — that's all I want to do. If you say fifteen, I'll go to fifteen; if you say thirty, I'll go to thirty. Whatever you want me to do, I'll do that.'

As time went on, I began training the people in the colony telling them that the only way in

He desperately wanted to reach out to them

which their health could improve was if they understand how to improve it themselves. I was only one person — they had to learn how to approach the government to get facilities from them. I explained Government policies to them and I used to take them with me to the Government officers and say, 'If you have a water problem this is the man you should approach.' I concentrated on women because they are the ones who bear the brunt of the problems in the slum situation. I trained them as community help volunteers and told them that for minor ailments they didn't need to come to a doctor. At the end of their six months training, they were totally transformed and were able to treat the sick and give advice about vaccinations, family planning and many different things.

I have put great emphasis on training and that is the reason we have such a large organisation, still happily functioning. I transfer skills not only to the people living in the community but also to the staff at all different levels. After ten years of working and training in the many communities the women are now so empowered that they run their community groups totally independently! I still see patients of course, but the main thing is to continue to train others because that's what has the multiplier effect.

Working in the slums has been tough and dangerous because all the criminals reside in these colonies. People used to scare me saying, 'How are you going to go into these places, you're a girl?' But I feel so empowered by God. There have been many times when the same people, to whom we give everything, emotionally, physically and in every way, abuse us and insult us. Sometimes we get so discouraged but for me, Jesus' life has been a supreme example of all of this. I always remember that the things he did were *only* good — nothing but good — and yet in return he was crucified and so I say, 'Lord, What is this? What we are suffering is nothing in comparison to what you went through.'

It is like flying at a very high altitude

I was never tempted by an easier or more lucrative job as a doctor because I have been sold out on Jesus from the beginning. I may have been discouraged at times but that discouragement is very short-lived and I always find that God has given me so much love for these people. I have learned that every problem the Lord brings is ultimately to glorify him because he has proved himself to be so mighty. I'm always praying 'Lord, let it not be an easy ride because I don't want my dependence on you to go down by even a little bit. Let it be tough — it doesn't matter — let it be so I'm always walking in faith, and I'll always come running to you like a child comes to a father.'

I shared with my associates recently that I have never gone to the Lord with a list of supplications for myself. Somehow, right from the time that I came into a relationship with him nothing materialistic like clothes or a beautiful house ever interested me, they were abhorrent to me. Just being in a position to help all these people has given me such joy and peace. And knowing that I've been able to do something small for God has been supreme — it is like flying at a very high altitude and everything else seems microscopic.

Jesus means everything to me. Because I was deprived of parents and a brother he's been a father, he's been a mother and he's been my brother. He also gave me many Christian brothers and sisters. So, what shall I say about a God who has provided me with a family? In this culture with arranged marriages we don't choose our own spouse, and the way in which God has given me a wonderful husband is in itself such an amazing testimony. I met Freddy at a mutual friend's wedding and it was fantastic. I never asked for him and it was as though God was saying to me, 'Don't worry about anything. I'll send your way, at the right time, what you need and what you want.' And I can only respond, 'Lord, how can I describe your faithfulness? Even if I write volumes it won't be enough.'

JUAN MALLEA
HIS PURPOSES ARE GOOD

From the start, 1993 was a monumental year for me. On 1st January my business was badly affected by a fire in the market where I sold clothing. Next, I had an accident, falling from the second floor of a house; I fractured my right hand, which required treatment for nearly three months. Then in March just after my thirty-fourth birthday, the car we had been relying on for our business gave up the ghost. We were forced to take stock and really think about what was happening in our lives.

Every month awful things seemed to occur so we asked God, 'Why have you been *allowing* problems to beset us in our business, with our car, and with our health as well? Everything has gone wrong for us, Lord, you have taken away our livelihood, all we have, we have nothing left to give you.'

When I was nineteen, I had made a decision to follow Christ but my Christian life had not been constant — it had alternated. Many times the Lord had to redirect my vision and I felt this might be the reason these things had been happening so I decided to repent and recommit my life to him.

In June, my wife Cristine's salary increased a little and this helped us to buy some things for our baby Juan Eliab. Life became better and we started to think that our difficult times had ended but on 10th July I was arrested and unjustly imprisoned.

Working as a taxi driver, I dropped off a passenger outside a particular house one night. A policeman approached and told me to get out of my car while he searched it. I had no idea what he was looking for and the only thing he found was my Bible.

He then took me into the house where there were a lot of people lying face down on the floor, with their faces covered. I had heard about people who just disappeared and the first thing I thought was that I must call my home and tell somebody what was going on. I invited the police to go to my house and search it as well but what I really wanted to do was to get them there so my family could know what had happened.

The passenger turned out to be a member of the Shining Path terrorist movement. They wanted to denounce the police because they had been blamed for the deaths of twelve students and a university teacher, and as this was untrue they were editing an illegal newspaper to put forward their side of the story. Because my passenger was not carrying anything, I had no idea who he was. He had just knocked at my door and asked me to take him to a house in my taxi.

The police took me to the station. I was not allowed to communicate with Cristine or a lawyer and was eventually told that I would remain there for fifteen days. I had met many people who had been tortured but never expected it to happen to me. I thought that it only happened to those involved in terrorism.

On 21st July at 2.00 am I was taken from my cell to an office by two policemen. There was a paper on the table sanctioning them to torture me. They said I was the author of a document found in the house, supposedly containing certain maps, which gave the locations of the bodies of people who had been killed in the past, twelve students and one teacher of the university. They were accusing me of something I did not do and they did not believe me when I protested my innocence — so began my torture.

> **There were a lot of people lying face down . . .**

Take care of our baby and . . . find me a lawyer

First, they used psychological means, telling me they were going to kill my wife and son, my mother and father, and then they said, 'We are going to kill you. If you want to live you have no alternative but to admit your guilt.' I refused to sign the paper they gave me.

They then started to beat me; they broke my teeth and one of my ribs. I kept telling them that I did not know anything about the documents or murders. Thinking it would help, I shared with them that I was a Christian. They said that they were also Christian, because they were helping society get rid of the terrorists. This provided me with an opportunity to continue talking to them, and fortunately it stopped them from hitting me anymore. Thanks to God, morning was nearly upon us, the torture session ended, but it had been a very, very long night!

The next day they took me to a press conference where they continued to lie about what I was supposed to have done. The press had done their own investigation and protested my innocence; they later published many reports in the newspapers, full of sarcasm towards the police for what they had done to me. They wrote that I was a Christian, and that all who knew me gave good reports of my character.

Meanwhile, Cristine, who was tireless in requesting help for me, went to the National Evangelical Council, and with my pastor's support, managed to get them to take my case. Meetings were arranged and people from several churches called for a public statement to be made about cases, like mine, where innocent people were unfairly put in prison.

The leaders from the Council were having some doubts because they knew that if they categorically stated that I was innocent, the media and police would criticise them. However, following a vote everyone was agreed that they had to make a public statement protesting my innocence. After that, the lawyers handling my case, and all those who had supported me, began to receive threatening phone calls from the intelligence services.

From the time I was arrested and taken to the police station, investigations took fifteen days. I was then moved for two months into a local prison attached to the Court. While there I was able, by bribing the guards, to see Cristine and my parents for the first time but it had to be done secretly. I was also able to give Christine some letters I had written. In one of those first notes I said, 'My dear Cristine, I hope you are well. You have to learn to trust in our Lord Jesus. Take care of our baby and please try to find me a lawyer. Do not stop smiling. God loves you very much, as do I.' Juan.

In the local prison I asked some Christians for help and this resulted in a special team supporting me. They gave me some Bibles and study material in order to work with other prisoners and that began my involvement in a work that would not have interested me when I was free.

At the end of the two months I was sent with some other prisoners to the Maximum Security Penitentiary Castro Castro. When we arrived we were forced by guards to lie face down on the floor while our possessions were checked. When they noticed that I had a Bible they questioned me sarcastically about it and myself. The Governor came by and one of guards said to him, 'Governor, here we have a man who professes to be a Christian.' The Governor asked if any more people were claiming to be Christians and four more identified themselves. We thought something nasty was going to happen to us, but the Governor said it was OK but he expected us to demonstrate it externally as well as internally.

Normal practice was to beat every new prisoner but the guards did not beat us, either then or in the future. As far as we know this was the first time that this had happened, so we thanked God for protecting us.

The Governor separated those who had already been sentenced from those yet to be sentenced, in which group I was placed. Those who had sentences of thirty-five or more years were then separated again. A new period thus began, and those of us who were Christians experienced at first-hand God's care for our lives.

We began each day with an hour of Bible study. Although we were in our own cells we could hear one another if we spoke very loudly. As time passed, many joined our group and came to know Jesus. That group grew and grew until today, literally, there is a church inside the Penitentiary.

Amazingly, we were asked to select a small group from among us to visit those serving life sentences. The guards took us to cells on another floor in the same building. Many of us were afraid that we were going to be killed or would be given life sentences ourselves. When we got there, some of prisoners jeered at us, challenging, 'Are you the ones from the other floor who sing? If so, please do continue!' I replied, 'OK, if you want me to sing, tell me what songs you like?' I sang what they requested and many of their faces changed.

We told them the story of David who killed his army captain Uriah, in order to have Uriah's wife, Bathsheba. Those with life sentences said that David was a bad person and was guilty because he had killed Uriah. I told them that, while this was quite true, they must not forget that David asked for, and received, the Lord's pardon. I sang Psalm 51 to them in which it says, 'Have mercy on me, O God, according to your unfailing love; according to your great compassion blot out my transgressions. Wash away all my iniquity and cleanse me from my sin.' They believed that because they had done such bad things, it was impossible for them to receive salvation. I told them this was not true because no matter what a man has done wrong, he always has the opportunity to draw close to God.

I believe God gave me the chance, in that dark place, to tell others about him and all that he has done for mankind. Those who shared this experience with me had been afraid, but we came to the conclusion that the Lord wanted us to share his love for these people. It was difficult to share with them because we knew they were guilty of many crimes but we did it anyway and at last we were able to experience much joy over what was happening.

When I was arrested, Cristine was four months pregnant and was now experiencing many problems with the pregnancy. Life was very difficult for her but she supported me every day by working and going to the organisation, Peace and Hope, and other entities to battle for my pardon. As news of our situation was made public she received sacks full of letters of encouragement from people all over the world who said they were praying for us, and that gave us hope!

Even the President of the Government Congress apologised directly to her because he knew that I had been imprisoned unjustly. My case had been evaluated and many things were coming to light. The police stated that the bodies they found in the locations shown on the map were indeed those of the murdered students and teacher of the university. Eventually it was discovered that the military was responsible and each one of the murderers was identified and judged.

The press, who had kept in contact with Cristine, began to ask the government and the authorities why I was still in prison when it was known that the military had committed the crimes. Many people demonstrated in front of the Justice Palace to protest, demanding that I be released, but the judge and the court still refused.

December came and we hoped that because it was a special time of year the authorities might show some sympathy and let me be released. I was still awaiting sentence and my lawyers were doing everything possible to avoid my coming before the faceless military court,

No matter what a man has done wrong, he always . . .

whose job was purely to pass sentence, without checking on the rights and wrongs of the case. It was a particularly difficult month for me because I wanted to be at home with my family and Cristine, who was due to have the baby.

We prayed that the Lord would take care of the birth and make the baby healthy, despite all the difficulties and hardships we had been through. On 10th December my family were to visit me; Cristine was about to leave the house to come to the prison, when she felt her first contractions. She went to the doctor who told her the baby was due in about eight hours. She really wanted to visit me in the Penitentiary during those eight hours, but the doctor advised against this and told her to go home and get some things together before going to the hospital.

The woman in the next bed, who was three months pregnant, had to stay in hospital because the doctors suspected a possible miscarriage. All the staff at the hospital were attending a meeting that day and nobody was available to help my wife with her labour. This woman turned out to be an obstetrician and helped Cristine give birth to a healthy baby boy whom we called Caleb. Later, Cristine told me that the woman had given her much better help than the doctors would have done. The next day she returned to the hospital to thank the woman, but could not find her. She only knew that her name was Isobel and although she tried to find her, she had disappeared. The Bible says that God sometimes sends his angels to take care of his children, and we believe now that this is what happened.

Christmas arrived, with people in the cells exchanging greetings and crying as they remembered their families. We asked the Lord to grant our families consolation. No pardon came for me, but on 28th December one of my brothers in Christ, who had been unjustly sentenced, was freed.

I was scared as it was forbidden

Saul, another brother in Christ, shared the same cell with me. He had been sentenced to twenty years in prison but he still worshipped and praised the Lord so I began to attempt to understand what God was trying to show me. I realised that when I had been free I had missed many opportunities to witness to others about Jesus so I prayed, 'Lord, if you want me to stay here, then I will stay. I will not pray for freedom any more but please help me to fulfil your purpose.'

At the beginning of 1994 I was becoming used to my situation and almost forgot about my own troubles because I became so involved with helping the other prisoners. The authorities told us that I had to wait six months before coming up before the *faceless Military Court* who would not try me but merely pass a sentence.

In April, out of the blue, someone came and told me that I was *free to go*! It was a very emotional moment because I had not been expecting to be freed. When I left that day Saul and I hugged each other and all I could tell him was that he was not going to be in there for ever. I encouraged him to continue working for the Lord and said that I would return to visit him.

The Lord put a burden on my heart for those who were in prison and in early 1996 I was able to go back to the Penitentiary again, as a visitor. I was invited to go by a group from Peace and Hope, the organisation who had worked hard for my freedom. For me this was very important, because it enabled me to go back and begin working on what I felt committed to.

Almost twenty months had elapsed since I had been freed. I wanted to see Saul, but I was scared as it was forbidden for an ex-prisoner to return to the Penitentiary. I was put in the middle of the group to prevent my being recognised. Once inside I had a fright when somebody shouted my name. It was not a guard but one of my old cellmates who had recognised me. I tried to indicate to him to be quiet but he did not understand!

When I reached Saul's cell the shock of seeing me made him fall down. I approached the bars, put my hands through, and talked to him. Many prisoners thought that I had been put back in prison and they did not understand that I was visiting them in the capacity of a counsellor.

Eventually I was able to obtain a pass from the authorities and have gone back many times to help those who have been unjustly sentenced. My case became a symbol to others as I was one of the first people to be released with a pardon; since then nearly 300 innocent people have been granted freedom thanks to agencies like ADOC, and Peace and Hope.

As a result of what has happened, our family is now a unit and these problems have helped us to become closer to each other. Life is very good for us now and we have a lovely daughter, Bicky, born on 27th June 1996. She is a big part of my life and has become a consolation to me because she has helped me forget many of the bad times in prison.

Cristine and I have learned so much through these terrible times. She is a different person now, she is brave and courageous and we have learned to commit everything into God's hands.

God is a God of justice and if he allowed me to be in prison it was because he had a purpose in it, and his purposes are good. God taught me that I should never forget him again. If I had not been in prison, I would not have learned the Christian life. God knew that I had a hard heart, so the lesson had to be hard.

Nearly 300 innocent people . . .

MICHAEL CASSIDY
AFRICAN ENTERPRISE

I was born in Johannesburg in 1936 and was an incredibly naughty little boy, quite notoriously so; people still remember me for my pranks and mischief!

When I was very small we moved to the British Protectorate of Basutoland. My father was an engineer in charge of the light and power of the territory. My mother was an outstanding pianist who went to the Royal College of Music in London.

I was politicised very early by our next-door neighbour, Patrick Duncan, the son of Sir Patrick Duncan who had been the Governor General of South Africa under Prime Minister General Smuts. Pat was a fanatical opponent of apartheid and when the Nationalists came to power in 1948, he convinced me that it was a tragedy. He was a passionate political activist, my childhood hero, and I admired him immensely. I had two strands running through me, one, an early political awareness that what our country and we were all caught up in, was terribly wrong, and two, a spiritual quest in the middle of schoolboy pranksterism. It was in that kind of posture that I went off to Cambridge University in England in 1955.

The very first Cambridge students who came to say, 'How can we help you?' were from the Christian Union. Although they came on other kinds of errands, they made it their business to share their faith. I told them I was a Christian and there was no way I needed any extra help. I think they rather despaired of me as a sort of a young Pharisee, whose religiosity, Anglican background and churchmanship would never make it possible for him to come to any clear conversion. But one day, a young Anglican law student, Robert Footner, took me off to Communion in the Round Church, which is an old Norman church.

After the service we went back to the College for breakfast. With twenty minutes to spare before the dining rooms opened Robert invited me up to his room. He was a man of few words, the kind of person who cuts past all the superficialities, subterfuge and camouflage. When the door was shut, he simply said to me, in a way that shocked me very much, and actually angered me quite a bit too, 'Michael, tell me something. Do you know Christ?' I was absolutely taken aback and somewhat offended. I replied, 'Well, I go to church. You can see that, and I do my best and so forth.' He was unimpressed with my answer.

He told me there were two very different things. To *know* Jesus Christ, or to know *about* Jesus Christ, as you could *know* the Queen of England, or know *about* the Queen of England — two very different realities. I had never ever heard language like this. It was very challenging and very shocking to me. While I was still trying to recover from the first question and make some sense of it, he put the second one: 'Michael, have you ever surrendered your life to Jesus Christ?' I knew what the term meant and I realised, with that question, that I had done everything in the religious life except that. I had been baptised, I had been confirmed, I had been an active communicant, I had given collection, I had a modest habit of reading a Bible and saying some simple little prayers. But this particular question sliced past that, to a question of my *will* and where was I in terms of my will? I realised that the one thing I had actually refused to do was surrender my will.

I was very much running my own life and deciding my own future, where I would live and what I would do. I was in charge. I was king and the crown was on my own head. This challenge broke past that. Still rather defensive and somewhat angry, I said, 'No, I don't think I have.'

It was very challenging and very shocking

There was tremendous love shining from Robert's eyes, and with a look of great concern and compassion he said, 'Well, you can do that, if you want to. In fact, you could even do it now and we could pray a little prayer. You could surrender your life to Christ.' He then went on to say, 'There's a little verse in the last book of the Bible, Revelation 3:20, where Jesus says, "I stand at the door and knock. If anyone hears my voice and opens the door, I will come in . . . You do your part, he'll do his.'

I remember thinking that if it wasn't true I had nothing to lose, and if it was true I had everything to gain. It was rather like Pascal's wager: maybe I should bet or wager my life on this step and on this response. He invited me to kneel there and then in his room, which was to me a totally extraordinary notion — to kneel with a friend in their bed-sitter and pray — this was going over the top in a big way!

I don't know how or what I prayed, or even if he led me in prayer, but I did understand this idea of surrender, a volitional response, and the Revelation 3:20 idea of asking Christ into my heart clicked and made some sense. So I took that step in prayer, in his room, and as I got up, his face was absolutely radiant. I thought to myself, 'He really is a bit of a nut, actually. This is all pretty wild and crazy. But anyway, I've done it and we'll see.'

I remember nothing about breakfast except walking across the quadrangle at St Catharine's College, looking up into the heavens and saying, 'God, Lord, if you actually are there and if this thing is real and is not a fake, I expect you to change my life.' I don't know what led me to that sort of boldness, but I continued, 'I have got to know. I want my life to be changed and I want it to be sure, I want it to be noticeable otherwise this will be it for me. I'm not fooling around. I am very serious about this thing and I think I've done my side, as I've been told by Robert and if you are there and the heavens aren't empty brass, then I want you to come to me and manifest yourself to me.'

My memory is blank for the next four or five hours of that Sunday, which was, I think, the 23rd October 1955. However, by mid-afternoon, I was suddenly aware of a presence that I had never ever known in my life. I couldn't describe it, but its reality was unquestionable and there was a severe sense of the presence of God. I found myself saying, 'I know you. I know you, Lord. I have met you Lord. I have encountered you, Lord. You are for real. This is what Robert meant when he said, "Do you *know* Christ?" And I've only ever known *about* you, and now I *know* you and you've come to me.' It was mind-boggling, I was incredulous, and the whole thing overwhelmed me. And, with my particular type of temperament, it manifested itself in an enormous sense of excitement.

That night, at the evening service at Holy Trinity Church, I don't remember much about the sermon but I remember the blessing at the end when the minister said, 'The peace of God, which passes all understanding, keep your heart and mind in Christ Jesus.' I said to myself, 'For the first time ever, I understand that blessing.' I suddenly became, overnight, a firebrand at college, to the point where nobody quite knew what to do with me. I frightened the daylights out of everybody. I testified to everybody. In fact, that same night, I cycled round at high speed to a friend from South Africa, burst into his rooms and told him, 'I've found Christ!'

Christ became real to me very, very quickly and I was excited beyond measure. My dear friends in the Christian Union introduced me to Christian literature for which I have always been thankful. One of the books was called, *The Cambridge Seven* by John Pollock. He wrote about C. T. Studd and a number of other Cambridge students who had a great impact on China. Out of all their witness and work came the China Inland Mission. On the last pages of the book, which riveted and gripped me, John Pollock says, 'This is the story of ordinary men and thus may be repeated.'

> **This was going over the top in a big way!**

I was staggered, challenged and overwhelmed by that, and I thought that if there was an adjective to describe me, 'ordinary' would be it, and if God could use an ordinary person, then I could be a candidate. So I immediately said, 'If you can use ordinary people, then here I am!' Although I was planning to be a schoolmaster and had just changed my course from law to languages, I nevertheless felt that somehow or other I wanted to be a witness to this Christ.

Very soon after my conversion, I had the experience of my bicycle being stolen. In Cambridge everybody operated on a bicycle and to lose it, caused great problems. I was upset about this, but I had been converted. I had a Lord, Saviour and Heavenly Father. So I said to the Lord, 'I want you to get my bike back by Wednesday evening, 7.00 pm.'

I told Robert and other Christians in the college: 'I have asked the Lord for my bicycle back. I'm giving him a few days.' Robert said, 'You can't ask him things like that!' 'Why not?' I asked. The mature Christians were appalled. I was passionate and terrified everybody out of their wits when I came near, and they all said, 'What are we going to do? He's asked for this thing by 7.00 pm on Wednesday. What's going to happen if it's not there? He's going to be so shattered and devastated!'

On the Wednesday night I was late for the College dinner and they shut me out saying I must come to the second session. All the time I was thinking, 'Lord, we're in countdown time now. It's 5.30, 6.00, 6.15. I don't know, God, how you're going to do it.' The Christians unbeknown to me, were in a state of crisis! As I was locked out of supper and had about 45 minutes to spare I decided to visit a South African friend who lived close to the College, down a very dark lane. 'Hello Pam, I've just popped in before supper to tell you about my bicycle and have you pray with me that I'd find it. The Lord's got about twenty minutes to get this thing back.' She was about five or six years older than I and was mature in the faith. She said, 'I don't know how you can do this Michael. It's not the sort of thing you can ask.' 'Why not? I mean, He's Lord. He's in charge. He's all-powerful,' I responded. She wrung her hands in despair, like everybody else. I said, 'Well, I must leave for College. It's ten to seven. The Lord's got ten minutes. The Dining Hall opens at 7.00 pm.'

I walked back down the dark little narrow lane towards my College and as I walked, the moon came out like a shaft of light and it glinted on metal. I went over and there was my bicycle! Nine thousand bicycles in Cambridge, and it was my bicycle! At 6.55 pm! I rolled up in front of the other guys. 'Hello, chaps. Praise the Lord. He's found my bicycle in a dark alley!' They laughed, of course, like Abraham and Sarah!

Shortly after that, Billy Graham came to Cambridge. I had never heard evangelism like that before and he became an instant hero. I decided I should go to Seminary in America so in 1957 I went to New York. The only Christian I knew of in the whole of the United States was Billy Graham. I had shaken his hand once, so I wrote to him. My letter went to the Crusade Office and because there were dozens of mailbags coming in, they had teams of students helping to sort the mail. A Japanese student from Fuller Seminary read my letter, rang me up, and invited me to the Crusade at Madison Square Garden.

After attending a number of times I felt the Lord saying to me, 'I want you to do evangelism like this, in the cities of Africa.' It was such a clear word it almost knocked me over, and here was I planning to be a little schoolmaster in a preparatory school. I was terribly nervous of anything in public, public speaking, even coping socially, and so it was frightening to have this call from the Lord! I said, 'No. You don't make mistakes too often Lord, but this once you've got it wrong!' To cut the long story short, I made application to Fuller Seminary for entry and a scholarship, both of which came in due course.

MICHAEL CASSIDY

You can't ask him things like that!

MICHAEL CASSIDY

The cheek of it! The nerve of it . . .

At the end of 1959 I was asked to give my testimony at the Seminary. Charles Fuller heard it and said, 'I've never had this sort of leading before with a student, but I want to help you get started in Africa. I'll make available secretarial help and a little financial help, and you can produce a leaflet, and here are two or three people, friends of mine, to form the nucleus of a Board.'

I had no idea what to call it, and when a friend said he'd heard of a ship that travelled between Africa and the US called *African Enterprise*, I thought, 'Sounds nice. Doesn't give away too much. It doesn't sound too overly-religious and it has a nice ring to it.' The work was born!

I began slowly to build up a group of people who would pray and give, and in 1961 the way opened for me to travel around Africa. I visited political leaders, church leaders, missionaries, evangelists and others, and as I did so the sense of calling to the cities of Africa as a focus, emerged. Indeed, the first invitation for a citywide mission in South Africa during the following summer of 1962 came from a place called Pietermaritzburg where we now live.

That summer five of us went back under the name of African Enterprise, and conducted our first campaign, which was wonderfully successful. The City Hall was jammed to capacity for two weeks and it had never before been filled for more than three days. And we were just kids! The cheek of it! The nerve of it, when I look back! But the Lord owned it. That was the glorious thing about it. It was his, and he transformed this thing from just an embryonic, loose, maybe airy-fairy, vision into something of substance and reality.

I finished my training, got the Board functioning, and left for Africa in late 1964, beginning public ministry the following year. The mission statement of African Enterprise, as we put it now, is *to evangelise the cities of Africa through word and deed in partnership with the church*. We immediately began to work with the church. Even before we had that mission statement we saw our responsibilities as holistic, word and deed, not just focusing on the proclamation of the gospel, but relating it contextually and to society. In the South African context, of course, that meant facing up to the apartheid challenge, which put us on a collision course with the State, the security police and even with a lot of people in the white evangelical church.

We were very clear from the start that the ministry of Reconciliation was not just to be reconciled to God but also to be reconciled to one another. The work developed and we now have ten teams across Africa.

In South Africa we were face to face with probably the most notorious and evil form of racial discrimination ever devised. Trying to bring a testimony into that environment was particularly difficult because the mainline churches, whose theology was perhaps less evangelical than my own, were the ones with whom I could identify on the social and political issues. The more evangelical churches, with whom I shared a basic theological and biblical posture, were either explicitly or implicitly supportive of the South African status quo, or of the apartheid system. That meant we were always caught between the forces of different sectors of the church. Because we had committed ourselves to work with the church, the Lord built up, through African Enterprise, a credibility with the overall body of Christ that enabled us to be meaningful and relevant unifiers and quite a strong catalyst towards unity. We were used by the Lord to help sponsor and facilitate several of the major inter-denominational conferences of the last quarter century in South Africa.

The first one was in Durban in 1973 when we brought together 800 leaders. We had enormous opposition from the South African Government, even to the point of them blocking all the twenty-five overseas speakers we'd invited, including Billy Graham. We had to pray that decision into reversal, and they finally granted permission.

That was a very seminal happening because the church came together and evangelicals learned from the ecumenical crowd about the socio-political concern and horizontal concern, and the ecumenical activist crowd learned about evangelism and the evangelical faith from the evangelicals. I think the South African church, after this event, became much more holistic, much more relevant, much more biblical in many ways.

In early 1977, the Chairman of our Uganda Board was murdered by President Idi Amin and our team was thrown in the deep end with the Uganda convulsion because our team leader, the famous Bishop Festo Kivengere, became the next No. 1 target. He had to flee, with many Ugandans, down to our office in Kenya where we found ourselves in a terrific project of social and practical concern and a very strong aid and development component came into our work. It was very demanding and costly for our team to face Idi Amin.

In 1978 there was a bush war in Zimbabwe and the black liberation fighters, whom the whites called terrorists, were fighting against the white tradition army to secure independence for old Rhodesia. Again we were trying to minister to politicians, get people together, challenge the church to face up to its role, etc. The following year we repeated the Durban conference exercise in South Africa but this time with 6,000 leaders from forty-three denominations coming together. That, in my view, was a critical moment in South African Christian life and history. It was a moment when the apartheid monolith began to be cracked and again, people learned from one another on different sides.

Many relationships were formed, which have remained to this day. However, it was very, very tough. We had opposition from people in the churches, who should have known better, from the Government and from the security police. It was hard for me personally, because white evangelicals used to say, 'Oh, no, we don't like Michael or support Michael because he's political.' The idea was that to oppose apartheid was political, whereas to support it explicitly or implicitly was not political. I never could figure out the logic of that.

We had to face the situation in Rwanda. Our team leader, a brother called Israel Havugimana, was a Hutu who challenged the government with its injustices against the Tutsi people. When the Tutsi Liberation Army began coming back at Rwanda it looked very menacing and threatening and the Hutu government reacted by killing Tutsis and people who were opposing them. The real convulsion came in April 1994 when a plane, carrying the two presidents from Rwanda and Burundi, was blown out of the sky. The Hutu militia went crazy, and our team leader and his family were lined up and shot. Many others in our team and Board were among the million people who died in that genocide. Since then, we've been involved in a reconciliation type of initiative to see the healing of Rwanda.

In August of 1992 we launched a project called Harambee '92 whereby we celebrated thirty years of our ministry since that first mission in Pietermaritzburg in 1962. We brought forty colleagues from the rest of Africa together, had some celebratory meetings, and travelled round the country ministering to and praying for various political leaders. We began to feel that many of these leaders were closer to each other than they realised, although there were still tremendous gaps.

As a result, we felt we should try to get some of these politicians together to meet one another at an informal level. So at the very end of 1992, and through 1993 we mounted a series of dialogue weekends for politicians at a game lodge called Kolobe Lodge just north of Pretoria out in the bush.

Over six different weekends, we brought together about ninety top politicians, from the far left to the far right. They were encouraged in a three-fold process: firstly, to share their personal

It looked very menacing and threatening

stories and autobiographies, secondly, their vision for a new South Africa, and thirdly, the steps toward the achieving of that vision. To start with there was great tension with one another, people came with their bodyguards, people came armed with revolvers, one group came with AK47s — it looked as if we were going to have a major shoot-out! But we saw this as a talking experience, and the chemistry of dialogue and personal interchange in a relaxed environment worked miracles of transformation in terms of people's relationships. Out of this some astonishing relationships were formed.

As we moved towards 27th April 1994 when our first non-racial elections were to take place, it appeared as if the country, at one level, would be going from bad to worse and heading into civil war. Mandela was out of prison. The black liberation movements were free to function and it was a very highly charged political atmosphere. In spite of it being positive because it looked as if apartheid was going to end, it was also the worst of times and the country seemed as if it was going to unravel, with the tensions of trying to get this thing together.

The Government itself was desperate about the situation and there were unbearable tensions between the two major black groups, the African National Congress of Nelson Mandela, and the INKATHA Freedom Party of Chief Mangosuthu Buthelezi. So desperate was the situation that Mandela and Buthelezi invited an international mediating group led by Dr Henry Kissinger and Lord Carrington to come in. This was only twelve days or so before the elections, and within forty-eight hours the initiative had collapsed!

Kissinger says we are going to have Armageddon

We had decided to take an initiative ourselves and had brought into the equation Professor Washington Okumu, from Kenya. He had a long experience of behind-the-scenes diplomacy and although he had known Buthelezi and Mandela before, we gave him the network of relationships we had built up through the Kolobe Lodge meetings. He met a lot of the people, and we brought him into South Africa for several visits so he had the whole situation at his fingertips in a way that nobody else did.

Just before Kissinger and Lord Carrington came, Mandela and Buthelezi invited Washington Okumu to be an adviser to the International Mediators group. We were very thankful for that so you can imagine my distress when round about 14th April, Washington rang me from Johannesburg and he said, 'The whole thing has collapsed after forty-eight hours. Kissinger is going home. Carrington and all the other mediators are going home, and I'm going home to Nairobi. It's all over; Kissinger says we are going to have Armageddon. We're going to have one of the biggest catastrophes of the twentieth century.'

All the world's journalists had been descending and coming out of Bosnia to get ringside seats in South Africa to watch the latest cataclysm. I felt a very strong constraint in my heart when Washington said he was going home to say, 'Washington, you can't. We've invested far too much in this thing for you to go now and what other hope do we have? You know the ropes. You know the situation. You've got the insights and you've got the contacts. I feel you should soldier on, even if it's alone, to do what you can to try and bring the INKATHA Freedom Party and the ANC sufficiently together so that the election could go forth without war.' To his very great credit, maybe his eternal credit, Washington agreed to stay.

The story of what happened in those next few days from about the 14th to the 19th is very, very remarkable. He soldiered on alone. We were backing him in prayer and he was operating the linkages we had given him. As he did this, he began to formulate a plan that could bring these two sides together. (A dimension that I should not miss out on here is that all this was happening against the background of an incredible amount of prayer in our country. We had the privilege of forming a prayer chain of people to pray day and night, twenty-four hours a day, seven days a week, for two years.) We had called for a 'Jesus Peace Rally' in the Kings Park Rugby Stadium in Durban on 17th April. With all the tension, danger, and buses being fired on by opposition groups we thought that nobody would come. Between 25,000 and 30,000 people turned out for that prayer meeting!

Washington Okumu had agreed to meet Buthelezi but just before the meeting Mandela called him and said, 'I want you to come to Cape Town.' Buthelezi *did* come and in the VIP lounge, while 30,000 people were praying outside, a peace plan document drawn up by Washington was looked over by Buthelezi, Danie Schutte, President De Klerk's representative, and Mandela's representative Jacob Zuma, who was the Head of the African National Congress in Natal. They all felt that it had some promise. By the end of that evening, after everything else had failed, the major parties began to come together on this plan!

On Monday 18th the i's were dotted and the t's were crossed and on Tuesday, 19th April, De Klerk, Mandela and Buthelezi went on public radio and said that the elections could go ahead in peace.

Peace broke out within our country in a way that brought a holy hush to the newsrooms of the nation and in many ways, around the world. People used the word, 'miracle' to describe it. One newspaper had a headline, 'The day God stepped in to save South Africa'. *Time* Magazine said, 'History has thrown up an authentic miracle'. In the British House of Commons one of the MPs said, 'If there are political miracles in history, this is one of them.' The *Wall Street Journal* ran a headline, 'God and politics'. Editorial after editorial used the faith language of 'miracle.' *And peace came across our nation.*

The elections were held six or seven days later, and we had the four most peaceful days probably in the history of our country in terms of any form of crime. Up until then, it was mayhem. In our area alone, between fifteen and twenty people were dying daily — probably up to sixty dying each day throughout the country. It was horrific.

When I was overseas, a few weeks after that, journalists said, 'We don't understand what happened, because Kissinger came back saying Armageddon's about to happen, an apocalypse, and suddenly now, all these peaceful elections. What's taken place in the last nine days to change that?'

We knew God had intervened, and that led me to believe that no situation, whether it's Bosnia, Northern Ireland, Burundi, Rwanda or Israel and Palestine — and we've been involved in some of those situations — is insoluble by the Lord if the prayer price is paid.

I often think about it from where the Lord was. We seemed to be led to do this or that, and yet it seemed such a pathetic offering, so totally weak and so fragile. We had no money, no publicity, nobody was paying us any attention. The bigwigs were doing it all — Mandela, De Klerk, Kissinger and Carrington were leading, and so a few little guys running around talking about Christ and praying and helping people relate and understand each other seemed such a pitiful offering.

However, as I reflected on that I've often thought that maybe the Lord looked down from heaven and said, 'Look at this hopeless situation, let's see where we can find the weakest, most hopeless peace endeavour, and let me confound the wisdom of the wise and strength of the powerful by using that.' I think he looked at our little effort and said, 'That's feeble and weak enough. That's something I can use.' In the end, we had built that little fragile bridge in terms of some of those relationships and the Lord decided to take and use it in a way that was astonishing and humbling. I think that African Enterprise and I were very privileged to make a significant contribution in helping the breakthrough to happen.

Editorial after editorial used the faith language

MICHAEL CASSIDY

The role of De Klerk was historic and I think that he will have a very significant place in this story. His courageous initiative became the turning point of it all. De Klerk was the one who came to see that the way they were going with apartheid, pragmatically speaking, was not working. His decision to release Mandela, to un-ban the liberation movements including the Communist Party, and to set in motion a change of events, which would cost him his own power, was an incredibly bold political initiative.

There's no question that South Africa will always owe De Klerk and Mandela an eternal debt of gratitude. The challenges aren't over because South Africa has an ongoing culture of crime and violence, but the political breakthrough has been very real. The danger now is that we don't give thanks to the Lord for what he did.

South Africa will always owe De Klerk and Mandela

Miss ANCHALEE CHONGKADIKIJ
THE ONE AND ONLY

I became a star with my very first album! Overnight I became successful and everything I had wanted to be when I was a child had suddenly come true.

I was born in Bangkok on 15th November 1955 and share the same birthday as my father, but a different year of course! He was a famous journalist for an English newspaper, the *Bangkok Post*, and was its first editor. I adored my father because he was a real family man and used to talk to me. He loved music very much so I think I inherited my singing from him. My parents were not wealthy because having five children was expensive, so I felt that if one day I could be richer, I would be happy! As a teenager, I wanted to do something important, be someone famous — I did not know what I was going to do with my life, but I wanted to seek pleasure and be rich. To complete my education I went to University in America. I was in my first year when Mum rang to say that Dad had gone astray and left home. I was angry, very, very angry.

When I graduated, I came back home, started singing in hotels, drinking and having fun with friends. Like other Thais, I thought that life was something that just happened, with no particular meaning. So, I had a good time but could not find any real satisfaction. One day someone offered to write a song for me and to make an album. He told me that he wanted to make me into a famous singer. I replied, 'OK, I would like to try that.' Suddenly I found success, but deep within my heart, I felt empty — there was a big emptiness — and I did not know how to deal with that.

My first album, *The One and Only*, was released in 1985. It was very successful and resulted in many concert appearances, but as time went on the success started to decline. I had been drinking every day for many years, especially just before a concert. I was pretty much an alcoholic and, as well as that, I think I broke just about all of God's laws and even those of the Buddhist moral code.

I began to fear losing everything I had, so I started looking for something I could trust, but felt very frustrated and did not know where to turn. Then one day in 1990, one of my friends who was a new Christian came to see me and began to tell me about Jesus. One of my sisters was a Christian and had tried to tell us about Jesus twenty years earlier but we had never listened to her. This was the first time I really heard and took in that Jesus loved me, that he could be with me and that he was God. My friend told me that I could trust him and he could help me. I asked her how I could get to know Jesus. She said, 'You just pray and ask for his help.' That's all! So, that night I did what she told me. I did not know how to pray — my heart just cried out, 'Jesus, help me!' Just that! At that moment I felt something coming into my heart, something that overwhelmed me. I did not understand what was happening but I felt something warm, which touched my heart very deeply and I wept. Although I did not understand it, I knew that someone was in that room beside me. His love was so powerful!

Three months later at a Luis Palau mission in Bangkok my father responded to the invitation to give his life to the Lord. Shortly afterwards, my mother also gave her life to Jesus. They had been separated for nearly ten years but after they became Christians, they were reconciled and got back together again. I could not understand why my father had left and was very bitter. I loved him, but inside I could not forgive him. Eventually, before he died, I was able to forgive him when I realised that the Lord had forgiven me everything.

That night I did what she told me

MISS ANCHALEE CHONGKADIKIJ

I get teased about that all the time!

The first year I felt very excited about the Christian life. I wanted to spend every day reading the Bible and learning what God's plans were for my life. Every day God showed me something new and this was very exciting. I gave up my career at that time — it was not in very good shape anyway. I believed my Lord when he said that if I gave my life to him, he would take care of me, so I did not worry about my career or my fame any more. I just wanted to spend time with my Christian friends and learn more about Jesus. When I accepted Jesus Christ that night, I became a new person. I felt cleansed and clean again but I knew I had to change, which was a struggle. I still drank during the first year; even when I went to church on Sunday, I would drink a beer and then wash my mouth out. But I knew that they knew! I knew they could smell it! I could even smell it myself because the alcohol was in my body.

It took about a year and a half, before I could give it up and ask for help from Jesus to do this. One day I found I did not want to drink any more. I had come back from church after giving my testimony as to how God had helped me with many things, and yet I knew that I was still hiding this from people. I could not hide it from God so I asked him to forgive me and take it away from me. From then on, he gave me the strength to do it. Alcohol had harmed my throat and voice but I started singing Christian songs and leading the worship in my church anyway.

During the next four or five years the Lord healed me and gave me back my voice. Two years ago I decided to make a new album called *Crossroads* and everything came back, after ten years of absence! The tunes and the music on this album, although secular, are very easy to listen to and much softer than my first one. My old fans had been looking forward to hearing from me again so when it was released it was the talk of the town. My critics said, 'Oh, you can't come back now, it wouldn't be successful.' But we prayed, and thank the Lord it has been a great success.

The album that I hope to release next should express something of the love that I have experienced in Christ but I want non-Christians to listen to it too. I am currently working on my television programme called *The Answer to Life*. We have only one Christian programme here in Bangkok and it's on Sundays at 5.30 – 6.00 am every other week. We deal with all kinds of problems that people have, providing answers from the Bible, with some time given over to songs, hymns and testimony as well. We also hope to have a special programme at Christmas to present the true meaning of the season.

I live with my mum and sisters in Bangkok. I haven't married and I get teased about that all the time! But I'm happy — I have my three Yorkshire Terriers, my friends, my family and most important, my faith!

I grew up in a village in remote, rural Haiti. No running water, no electricity, and no roads — we used a donkey to go to town. When I was born on 20th September 1952, I think we were possibly the poorest family in the community. My mother had six children by my father and I was the youngest. When my mother was carrying me, my father had tuberculosis; he knew that it was a death sentence and that he would not see my birth. However, the Lord was gracious to him, he did see me born, and this is how he came to give me my name. When he saw me coming from my mother's womb he said, 'This is a gift of God. I did not expect to see this child so I will call him "This is a gift from God himself".' Dieumeme literally means 'God himself' but not when put in the context of my birth. My father died about a month after I was born, my mother then remarried, and that man died two or three years later. She thought she was going to be the exterminator of the male population in that particular village, so she took the vow of celibacy and would not marry again!

I can remember it as if it were today

My education and ABCs started with an uncle who could barely read and was known as 'unlefted'. Every day at devotions, my mother would recite memorised Bible verses like Romans 12:12 and because she could not read or write she was repeating the same thing over and over. One day she said, 'What I need is someone who can read the Bible, so that we can have a bit of variety in our devotional times.' She saw that I was interested in learning so decided to send me to the village school, about three or four miles from where we lived. She had no money but remembered that one of my older sisters had a rooster. She asked if she could borrow the rooster and told her that she would sell it so she could send me to school. The rooster was sold for US$1 and that was the tuition cost for the year.

I went to the village school for one year and then to a Grammar School in the town. It was a twelve-mile round trip every day and I had to do it on foot. Getting up early, my mother prepared a breakfast of plain white rice and oil and then by 6.00 am I was on my way to the town. She gave me two pennies for my lunch money.

I bought a piece of sugar cane for one penny, and used the other penny to pay for lessons to learn how to ride a bicycle. At 4.00 pm school finished and on the way home, particularly during mango season, I'd try to get some kind of a snack by using rocks to knock the mangos down from the trees. This was fun. I'd get home by 6.00 or 6.30 pm and try to study. One night I almost burnt the house down. I was studying, felt tired, lay down on my straw mattress and fell asleep. I must have knocked the lamp over in my sleep and was awakened by my mother frantically trying to put out a fire.

I became a Christian when I was twelve years of age through the ministry of my brother, who wasn't a pastor then. He was working at the main church in town and every summer they would send two or three people to outstations to teach Vacation Bible School. I can remember it as if it were today. He was teaching about sin and its consequences and explaining Romans 6:23 that says, 'For the wages of sin is death, but the gift of God is eternal life in Christ Jesus our Lord.' He said that we are all sinners and unless God takes care of our sins, then we will reap the wages of sin, which is death and hell.

You're joking, there is no chance

My brother is a very ardent evangelist and he said that with all the conviction that he could muster. I was keenly aware of the consequences of not responding to Jesus and having my sin problem taken care of. So, on the conviction of the Holy Spirit, I gave my life to Jesus. What I found meaningful after my conversion was that I had an appreciation of God as my Father. Because my father had died I had not known a father's love and care, but I now had a heavenly Father.

After seven years of Grammar School I thought that I was going to have a career in farming. One Sunday afternoon my brother said, 'Listen, you have to go to Port au Prince to take an exam to see if you can be admitted to High School.' I knew nothing about this but the next day I found myself in the Capital city for the first time; I took the exam, and passed. High School is seven years in Haiti, and the mission school I attended only had five of the seven years. At the end of the sixth year in the state school there was a Government exam — a French system called the Baccalaureate — and then, if that was successful, there was another exam at the end of the seventh year. Only after that was there opportunity to go to university. I looked at all the texts, which were being used for the fifth year, compared these books with the books for the sixth year, and found out that they were the same! So I thought, 'Well, knowing what I know, I'd better study them all and sign up for that exam.'

It's a tough Government exam and out of 50,000 people, only 3,000 would pass. It was that competitive. I told the school administrators that I wanted to do it and they just said, 'You're joking, there is no chance.' However, by God's grace I passed the exam, which meant cutting High School short by one year. When my brother saw that, he said, 'Listen, if you've come this far, then you have to do the last seventh year at another school.' The seventh year was much easier than the fifth year. Once the Baccalaureate 1 had been passed, then Baccalaureate 2 did not cause any problem, so having done that, I enrolled at the University of Haiti, Law School.

While studying Law I taught English and Spanish languages in some of the High Schools and also worked at the Radio Station as a News announcer, so life was very busy. I left the house at 6.00 am and did not get back until 9.00 or 10.00 at night, but I enjoyed it because I had a real passion to learn. I enjoyed Law — how I enjoyed it — and I was doing well there.

In my last year I was working for a Christian Radio Station, Radio Lumière when I received a call from an American who had come to visit Haiti. He came to see me and asked if I'd ever given any thought to studying the Bible in America. I replied, 'Oh no, no. I want to be a lawyer and I'm going to graduate in about ten months and begin my Practice.' However, he kept pursuing me, and my brother, whom I respect very much, encouraged me. His advice was, 'Well, why don't you just go. It won't hurt you as a Christian to have a degree in the Bible and to study Scriptures. Then you can come back, finish your Law and you'll have two degrees.' I decided to follow his recommendation — but I never came back to Law. I went to what was then the Detroit Bible College in Michigan to study for my Bachelor degree, and during the three years there, I fell in love with Theology. I also fell in love with Gloria, and we were married in 1979 after I graduated.

We moved to Chicago where I did my Masters and my PhD and it was clear to me that the Lord was leading me into the area of teaching or pastoral work. In 1984 I was pastoring a growing church in Chicago when we had a phone call inviting me to be Dean of a Graduate School in Jamaica. My response was, 'No, you've got the wrong man. I don't think I'm interested at all.' Nevertheless, he persevered, kept corresponding and eventually invited us to Jamaica at the end of 1985 just to have a look at things.

After about a year and a half we felt the call of God to Jamaica, although it was a tough decision, and started the work in 1987. In 1992 our sister school, the Jamaican Theological Seminary, was also looking for a President, so since then I have been serving as President of the two institutions.

The Seminary was struggling with few students and lack of recognition but we have seen God's blessings on the work. Both schools received accreditation by the Government and we now offer six programmes — two Bachelors, four Masters — to about 700 graduates from throughout the Caribbean. I am excited about the work of education and long to see not only our training of people for the church, but training people who can go back to their professions to penetrate society and be the salt and light of the gospel wherever they are.

Studying theology for so long has impacted me profoundly. In Haiti, our church was very strict and there was only one line apart from which nothing else could be true. Years of study showed me that this isn't the case. There are many areas for honest disagreements within the church as far as theology is concerned. People who are equally competent in their handling of Scripture and who are equally committed to Christ would disagree on things, so that made me much more tolerant of people who see things differently from the way I see them. Paul's statement in 1 Corinthians 13:12,13 — 'Now we see but a poor reflection as in a mirror; then we shall see face to face. Now I know in part; then I shall know fully, even as I am fully known. And now these three remain: faith, hope, and love. But the greatest of these is love', tells us that we will see much more perfectly. We see now through glasses, which are dusty and we don't even want to clean them because we enjoy the dust and want to see things our way. I have my own blind spots, my own prejudices, that colour my interpretation of Scripture and I have to be careful. Less arrogant, less confident in saying this is it, less dogmatic. However, in terms of commitment to the basic tenets of Scripture, to the basic tenets of evangelical faith, this has become much stronger and I think the years I spent in a liberal setting only strengthened my resolve and conviction in the authority of Scripture. I've studied the various challenges and theories that argue against it and don't believe they should lead us to doubt its authority. I try to be as faithful as I can to the major tenets of the faith — these we ought to hold on to, no matter what. There are certain things, which are essential to Christianity and I think this is very important in an age when an ideology of pluralism holds sway.

When I take the gospel to other cultures I want to allow it to speak with poignancy and sharpness. If the gospel, which is constant, is to address the different cultures with all its power, and to challenge in a very incisive way, then we must understand the culture. What transforms is not the *culture* of the missionary — the Word of God is what transforms. I speak with an accent and to some extent I cannot help having my cultural wrapping around the gospel, but I want it to be as thin as possible so that it doesn't cloud the good news. When I speak to people, I want them to hear the gospel, not my culture.

My schooling took twenty-eight years and started with the sale of my sister's rooster. This was, of course, the most profitable investment I have ever seen. My sister never forgets that this led to a PhD in Theology and so I have now been making payments on that rooster for about two and a half decades. I say sometimes 'Listen, give me the final bill for your rooster,' but she replies, 'No luck — you'll be paying for the rest of your life!'

I want it to be as thin as possible

BROTHER ANDREW
ALWAYS TRAVELLING — GOD'S SMUGGLER

My early life was uneventful. I grew up in a poor family in one of the smallest houses in a village north of Amsterdam. Never mind that it was almost opposite the house of the mayor!

I was only twelve or thirteen years old when World War II broke out and I felt it very keenly. It didn't take long before I was involved as a courier and doing little things with the Resistance Movement. I strongly hated and objected to the German presence in our village. I thrived because I could do *anything* — steal, provoke, little acts of sabotage like putting sand or sugar in the gasoline tanks of the German trucks — anything that was bad was seen as good, as long as it was anti-German.

In what we call 'the hunger winter' of 1944–45 we saw thousands of people walking, pushing prams or bicycles through our village on the way to farms and the north of the province trying to find food. Everything in my heart revolted — this is not right. It shouldn't happen. You've got to do something about it. And the spirit of resistance was awakened in me.

When the war was over, my first reaction was to fight to free Indonesia from the Japanese and re-establish Dutch rule. The fighting mood was in my blood so as soon as I was old enough to qualify for military service, I left my village and joined. I obtained a high level of training including commando-style silent killing, using only hands and knees to immobilise or kill just about anybody. This brought me to the forefront of the two specific fighting periods of which I was later to repent and deeply regret.

I knew in retrospect that what I had done was very wrong so I went back to Indonesia to ask forgiveness publicly. I did this several times, involving others and myself in mutual weeping. At the time though, I was enthusiastic and very patriotic and felt that it was something that had to be done, to avoid being a traitor to country and conscience.

Seeing the cruelties of war almost made me become a pacifist — I abhorred what I saw and did. Sometimes I would decide not to go out with the troops and they would come home badly wounded, with some killed. My blood would begin to boil and next trip, I would be there again, leading the guys, and fighting like mad.

In January 1949, at Jokja, a bullet smashed my right ankle. I was eventually flown to a Catholic hospital in Semarang where the Franciscan nuns took care of us in an extremely loving way. They were Dutch nuns and were old in our eyes but they worked with those beautiful young Indonesian nurses and that attracted us greatly. We experienced a caring that was out of this world, and it was there that a crisis began forming in my life.

Following the fighting near Jokja, I had not returned to the barracks. A friend of mine had to clean out my possessions and found, right at the bottom of my trunk, a Bible that my mother had given me in November 1946 when I left home. She had asked me to read it and I had said, 'Yes mother', because you never said, 'No mother'! But I didn't read it. My friend thought that perhaps Andrew would like this in hospital. Andrew did! I still remember him coming and giving it to me.

One day I approached my favourite nun, Patricia, and said, 'Now Sister, tell me how you can be so nice, so patient with us swearing, cursing, dirty-joke-telling soldiers.' We were just one filthy bunch in my opinion. 'How can you seemingly be on duty for twenty-four hours, never complaining,

I abhorred what I saw and did

always smiling, carrying out all our wishes, even buying us cigarettes?' The nuns did absolutely everything for us.

As I asked her this, her face became even more angelic, and she said, 'Andrew, it's the love of Christ within us!' That was the first time in my Dutch Reformed life, brought up as a Calvinist boy, that I heard a personal testimony about a different lifestyle due to the indwelling presence of Christ. That did not come into our Calvinistic teaching and it made me think. Receiving the Bible set in motion another change — and one thing led to another.

I arrived back in Holland in June 1949 on the hospital ship, still weak and limping. Evangelism, an unknown concept in Holland, was just beginning. I remember attending a meeting with a bottle of gin in my pocket, which was just about empty by the end of the service! But that was my life. I was not really interested but I knew there was something just out of reach, and I was determined either to find it, or to end my life.

There seemed no sense continuing with life — I couldn't take up my old profession as a blacksmith/engineer due to my injury. I had no faith; guilt and a bad conscience consumed me. After all we had killed 200,000 Indonesians, the kindest, most gentle people in the world — in a war that had been, in retrospect, political, similar to what the Americans became involved in a few years later in Vietnam.

That made me search and I can remember, when I arrived home in June, my family and father taking me that same evening to the cemetery to see my mother's grave. (A few months previously, in September 1948, I had received word, belatedly, that my mother had died and been buried. I didn't know my mother was dead and I was still writing to her until I heard from my oldest brother about the funeral. I was terribly upset.) I sat on a bicycle and they pushed it, because I was not yet sufficiently strong to walk the half kilometre necessary. I showed no emotion, but later that night I went back alone by using my bicycle to prop myself up. I threw myself on top of the grave crying, 'Mother, mother'. I was absolutely desperate, like a little child, but there was no answer, because mother wasn't there.

During that period I kept searching, kept reading the Bible, and one winter evening in our little village, in a small house, in the loft where I had my bed, I knelt for the first time, for my first *conscious* prayer. I can remember I said something like 'Lord, I don't understand it, but I want to believe. If you can show me the way, I will follow you.' That was my first prayer! I got up and felt no different — I did not know what to expect. But a few days later, converted people in the village said to me, 'Andrew, what has happened? There's something different about you.' I said, 'I don't know. Nothing.' Well, I was not aware of it but something must have changed that evening.

Six months later I was beside a dyke talking to God and feeling a kind of call that I had to be a missionary, but I said, 'Lord, I cannot. I have no education. I have not learned any languages. It's not in our tradition as a family or as a church,' but I came to the point of saying, 'Yes' and at that moment something happened to my smashed ankle. The moment I said 'Yes' I was healed and I knew it! I had always ridden my bicycle but that evening I decided to walk to a meeting without saying anything to the family. When they saw me leaving the house they thought I had changed my mind about going because it was four miles and too far for me to walk. But I walked!

I soon got involved in tent evangelism and a complaint I kept hearing was that factory workers and the low class did not go to church. My reaction was that if they didn't go to church, then the church must go to them and so I applied for a job in the largest factory in the region, a chocolate factory. I got a job as a labourer with the understanding of the Director-owner that I would evangelise. He was a very devout Christian so it was okay with him.

I threw myself on top of the grave

I worked in a department full of girls — about 200 of them. The dirty talk, the filthy jokes, the looks and remarks made me blush all day. They wouldn't believe that I had been in the army four years, but this was worse than the army. It was *terrible*! So after six months I went to see the Director and said, 'I'm leaving! This is not for me. It's too hard. I can't do it.' He said, 'Andrew, I'll give you one week to walk through the whole factory, look at every function and if there's anything at all that you would like to do, I'll help you to become that. It can be anything, except the owner!'

The Director wanted me to stay because he could see some influence and in fact a year and a half later, there was revival in the factory. Those dirty girls were singing hymns and reading the New Testaments that he had made available to me.

Around that time I got in touch with Worldwide Evangelisation Crusade — it had to happen! All they required was a love for Jesus, and a love for people. No intellectual requirements sounded very good to me. I arrived in London in April 1953 to study at this lay seminary and soon became a devout reader of Oswald Chambers.

One morning in May, the heading was 'Learning the habit of enjoying the disagreeable!' I had no idea what it meant really, but I thought it must be good if Oswald Chambers recommended learning it. Later that morning I was chosen to do the dishes in the WEC kitchen. There were stacks of plates, cups, saucers and cutlery. As I was battling through this pile of dirty dishes, a lady passed through the kitchen and said something like 'Do you mind doing the dishes?' It must have been in simple English although I didn't know what she meant, but I knew the answer. I said, 'No, I'm just here learning the habit of enjoying the disagreeable!' She stood there. Her mouth fell open. I mean this guy could hardly speak English and he came out with this big sentence, just like that! I consider Oswald Chambers to be my spiritual mentor, and the person who most shaped my Christian life and thought.

While in missionary training in Glasgow, I planned my first trip to Eastern Europe, in July 1955. I did not tell WEC anything about my trip to a Youth Festival in Warsaw. It was a real eye-opener. I often ask myself, why did I pick up a glossy magazine about the Communist youth festivals? Why not somebody else who would have simply thrown it away? I saw fantastic pictures and read fantastic stories about tremendous demonstrations. We're talking about hundreds of thousands. The biggest youth organisation in the world — 93 million members! Huge festivals all over the world! And I'd never heard of it.

The next one was going to be in Warsaw, Poland. So I wrote them a letter and said, 'I'm a Christian, I've read about you and I want to come. If you allow me to come, I will come, but I will act as a Christian.' They wrote back and said I was most welcome!

Revolution! That was their message! We're going to conquer the world! We will change the world! Big red flags! Parades! I heard the revolutionary cry that the West had never heard and there was no one to witness. No one! Because there was not one single mission working in the communist countries in 1955. I stood there by the side of the road with my Bible. Alone! And God spoke to me. 'Every knee shall bow, every tongue confess that Jesus Christ is Lord.' I looked at these people and I cried. Then I thought, 'Your knees will one day bow before my Saviour, but God give me a chance to share Jesus with you.'

On that first day that I wrote a very stiff letter to WEC, almost accusing them, telling them off, berating them, that they had educated us in a cloistered atmosphere. 'You don't know about the world outside of Christianity. You call yourselves the Worldwide Evangelisation Crusade but you only refer to half of the world. You are not in the other half. You're not interested; you have no vision; you've never been here!' And I thought, 'Well, they're going to be mad at me now!'

Revolution! That was their message!

**You have to
go after him to
get it back!**

In Glasgow they never let us go into the Gorbals and those other horrible places. I wrote that letter fearing reprisals, but I was surprised. They underlined my strongest statement and pinned it on the notice board and from that day on, students were allowed to go to the slums, the pubs and the gambling halls!

I had to go to the Headquarters in London and explain my actions — John Lewis, who died recently, said, 'Well, Andrew, as long as the Lord keeps the doors open, you shouldn't even consider applying for WEC membership. Carry on as you are — planning nothing, but saying "yes" at the right time.'

After that, I travelled a lot on my own, preaching and smuggling Bibles into communist countries and eventually, after returning time and time again, others joined me. People became aware of the work I was doing so 'Open Doors' was born.

My book *God's Smuggler* was published in 1967, twelve years after my work had begun. One of my strongest encouragers on the book was Mrs Chambers. She always said, 'Andrew, you *must* write a book about this.' I wasn't keen on the idea. But when Richard Wurmbrand's book, *Tortured for Christ* was published, it hit the Christian world like a bombshell. There was a reaction of fear and hatred towards Communists and that, for me, was a decisive factor in agreeing to write my book. I told my story to John Sherrill who wrote three articles in *GuidePosts* magazine. That was the big breakthrough. Following publication of the stories we invited people to contribute towards Bibles for communist countries by sending money to the American Bible Society. There was a tremendous response to this appeal, which still continues.

'Open Doors' has been described as combative, confrontational and controversial. If you're not going to stick your neck out, you'll get nowhere. I do break the law! Hallelujah I do! I'd get nowhere if I didn't break the law, but for every human law, there's a higher law — God's law — and everyone in leadership will one day have to choose between man's law and God's law. If you keep one, you have to break the other.

My second book, *The Ethics of Smuggling*, was written because people didn't know what went on in the Resistance Movement during the war. The thief is not the rightful owner of the thing he steals. You have to go after him to get it back! Apply that to nations, to persecution, to Communism, to Islam, to sects, to 'isms'. It makes you militant. Thus, in Christian terminology, you are confrontational or combative. I say, go after them! If a nation has no Bibles, or preaching is not allowed, don't accept that! Jesus says *'All nations'*! (Matthew 28). No one has the right to say, 'But not in my nation'.

Recently our new President Johan Companjen was at a conference with various mission leaders. Somebody asked him bluntly, 'What is the raison d'être of Open Doors? How would you describe it in one word?' He said, 'Presence. We are there.'

And that is what I want our one word to be — PRESENCE. If an invitation comes to teach in the Hamas University on the true meaning of Christianity, I hesitatingly, very hesitatingly, accept that kind of invitation, because I'm not a teacher, I'm not an intellectual, I'm not a lecturer, or a professor. But I'm there. I do it! I'm just a nobody; I have always been an employee in 'Open Doors'. They let me go and do my thing but with fear and trembling, because they get too much coverage as far as the Muslim fundamentalists are concerned. But we say, 'Why wait until there are terrorists on our doorsteps? We need to reach them *now!*'

Billy Graham proposed another Pastors' Congress in Amsterdam in the year 2000. I guess he sent letters to many thousands of people. One of my colleagues received one and I suggested the answer was 'It would be great to have another Congress, providing you put

Islam on top of the list because now it is still a *challenge*, but if we do not meet the challenge, it will become a *threat*.' That's my view.

In terms of numbers, they make up a quarter of the world's population; in terms of influence, they are the biggest influence; they scare everybody. People are very upset in Holland. They say, 'Andrew, look at how many churches in Holland are being bought by the Muslims and converted into mosques. It's terrible!' I reply, 'No. It is not terrible at all. What is terrible is that you have stopped going to church any more. The churches are empty and that is what's terrible! We are wrong, not the Muslims. They only use the opportunities that present themselves. *We* are wrong in that we are not crowding the churches. Then there would be no empty churches for the Muslims to buy.'

Our message is to the Christians — and our love, an inviting love, to the Muslims is to come and meet Jesus. So I say everywhere, 'Muslims have not rejected Jesus. They haven't seen him yet.' Wherever you go, to deportees, refugee camps or terrorist bases, you may be the first of Jesus' followers they've ever seen. I have had a great response from the Muslim fundamentalists. Embarrassingly so! So I go there and I say to our people, 'If you see a guy with a gun, don't run, don't preach, but go close to him, put your arm around him, because then he cannot shoot any more. For shooting, you need distance. But with your arm around a guy with a machine gun, he cannot shoot you!' I mean that, literally, and spiritually.

By failing to confront our own sinfulness with the redemptive power of Jesus to change a life, we don't have the guts to face up to threatening movements. By failing to ask forgiveness and cleansing, we fail to confront all the evil powers. We cover them up and therefore we have no moral guts to face an evil world.

I sometimes pray from the private devotions of Bishop Andrewes — that name appeals to me! 'Forgive me my sins, Oh Lord. Forgive me the sins of my youth and the sins of my age. The sins of my soul and the sins of my body. The secret of my whispering sins, my presumptions and my crying sins, the sins that I have done to please myself and the sins that I have done to please others. Forgive me those sins, which I know, and those, which I know not. Forgive them, Oh Lord. Forgive them all, of thy great goodness.'

Based on that prayer, I have noted a statement by Spurgeon: 'There may be persons who can glide along like a tramcar on the rails without a solitary jerk, but I find I have a vile nature to contend with. The spiritual life is a struggle with me. I have to fight from day to day with inbred corruption, coldness, deadness, barrenness, and if it were not for my Lord Jesus Christ my heart would be as dry as the heart of the damned.' Next to the statement, I wrote a little note, 'No wonder he was such an effective soul winner.'

I know I cannot live without the Lord Jesus Christ because there is no life without him. I want to be his friend and I want to talk to him, I want to walk with him — there are only a couple of people in the whole Bible of whom it is said, 'He walked with God.' One day when I was visiting the Oswald Chambers family I spoke to a neighbour about Mrs Chambers. She said, 'Every afternoon she goes out of the house to the post office with her arms full of little parcels of books to mail to all her friends world-wide.'

The neighbours would say, 'There goes Mrs Chambers, *walking with God*!' That's terrific — mailing your parcels, walking with God. This is what I want! I don't want a name, or fame, I don't even want to be 'religious'. I want to be a very down-to-earth person who walks with Jesus and can talk with him and tell him everything, and hear him speak his words of forgiveness first. If I can't firmly grasp the base of that total forgiveness and have 'him' growing in me, with the 'me' getting smaller, then there's no hope for me.

There goes Mrs Chambers, *walking with God!*

BROTHER ANDREW

I have worked in restricted countries for over forty-three years and many people now come to me and say, 'Andrew, if you had known everything, would you have done it, or would you do it again?' And I say, 'Definitely not! No, if I had known everything, I would not have done it. God in his goodness and grace, doesn't show you the end of the way. Sometimes he barely shows you the first step but he gives you the strength for each step as you walk almost in the dark.' That's how it's gone in my life and, I suspect, in the lives of many Christians.

I don't like travelling! Basically I think I'm a family man but it didn't work out because I was always travelling. The only time I took the whole family with me was on a trip to America. Talking with my wife Corrie on the plane — it must have been our 20th Wedding Anniversary — we calculated that of the twenty years, I'd been away ten years. The children all arrived in the first ten years; all five of them, and when they needed me, I wasn't there, and it just caused me great heartache. So a few years ago, I called them together and I confessed my sadness that I hadn't been there for them. The first years we were very poor and so it was always difficult. I only came home when I was too sick, dirty or poor to continue travelling. So I was never a pleasant father. I confessed my sin with tears and asked them for forgiveness. My oldest girl said, 'Oh, Daddy, we never missed you!' I replied, 'Now, you're making it worse!'

It just caused me great heartache

RUTH MEAKINS

I didn't cover my head like all the other women, so when a water engineer from England called Andy Meakins spotted me he came over and introduced himself. I spoke English so I could communicate with him and that helped build our relationship.

I was working on the same irrigation project as Andy near Addis and we lived in the same compound. As the church was a long way from where we lived, we used to walk there together and became good friends. One day he told me that he wished our relationship could be more than just a friendship. You may laugh about this! I was not very mature; I was only seventeen. His Christian life was very attractive but I didn't like bald men! I didn't want to hurt him so I said, 'No. I've prayed about it and the Lord hasn't said yes!' He responded 'OK, I've had confirmation from God that you are the one he is giving me, but if you say no, I'll wait and see!' I was silly at that time.

He eventually went back to the UK for Bible College and I went to college to gain some accounting experience. When Andy returned after five years I had matured and when he asked me again, I said yes, because I could see from his life what a good Christian he was; his life really demonstrated Christ.

Because of that, I blamed the street girls

We married in 1987 in Ethiopia and went to the UK for a blessing in his church. When we returned I started work with the Mineral Resources as a cost accountant. I had a very difficult time being accepted in local society in the first year of marriage. When an Ethiopian woman is with a white man, she is like a prostitute because the street girls look for foreigners to go out with. Whenever we went to a restaurant or hotel I could feel the eyes of our older people on us. I was not accepted and because of that, I blamed the street girls. I hated them.

We were living in a small apartment near the airport, in an area where a lot of foreigners lived, and where there were large numbers of girls around the streets. In 1989 when I was pregnant with Caleb, God showed me that Jesus had died for these girls as well as me. He wanted me to love them and share with them what I had. I said, 'No! That must be from Satan!' I shut off my mind and refused to listen. However, it kept coming so I shared it with Andy who said, 'If it's from God, it will stay and if it's from Satan it will go, so let's pray about it.' We prayed and prayed and it kept coming again and again, and not only was it coming to my mind, but whenever I saw these girls I started feeling love for them instead of hate. But I went to England to have Caleb and after that, I was busy with my baby.

When Caleb was two years old, we went to Manchester so that Andy could undertake two years of study to change his job from Water Development to Urban Development. Lydia, our second child, was born there. During that time in Manchester the Lord took me to where these street girls were standing and I said, 'Lord, I can't do this. Why are you bringing me to this area? Why do I keep seeing these girls? It's not my country, it's not my culture.' We returned to Ethiopia and I still felt concern for the girls.

After the arrival of Abigail, our third child, I met two girls, an Ethiopian and an American, who told me that they had the same vision as I did for the street girls. They had gone out the previous Thursday night and just drove around saying hello. They asked me to join them so the next week I fed my baby and gave her to Andy and he prayed, 'Bless us and send us.'

I hope Daddy's all right

On our way we prayed so many times, because it was dark and I was scared. I invited two girls to come and sit in the car and as they talked, I was overwhelmed and in tears; I said to the Lord, 'I know that you want me to help these girls.' After that we went out every Thursday until midnight and witnessed to them. When they came to the Lord the verse God gave me was, 'But seek first the kingdom of God and his righteousness, and all these things will be given to you as well.' I took that verse and shared it with them and the girls challenged me saying, 'If you want us to stop this work, to leave the streets, how do we survive and earn money to feed our parents?' I had done a two-year course in tailoring and sewing and thought, 'Why don't I use that?'

I went to a local mission and asked permission to use eight of their sewing machines. When they agreed we got everything ready and I taught the girls how to make curtains, waistcoats and kids' clothing. For support, we gave them money so they could buy bread and what they needed. Volunteers joined us but because the demand was very high, I totally neglected my family and that was a big problem. We then hired someone else to teach the sewing and tailoring and I became a counsellor three mornings a week.

About a year earlier, Andy had wanted to go to Nairobi, Kenya for a meeting on urban ministry. I didn't want him to go because we had never been separated and always went to things together. However, the previous week I had been on a silent retreat and when I returned home Andy said, 'You've had your retreat. Let me have mine.' I agreed.

Andy was supposed to go on Sunday but for some reason the schedule changed and someone suggested that he tried Saturday. He tried hard to get on the plane and called until 11.00 o'clock that night. In the morning he took our passports from the cupboard and gave me mine saying, 'This is your passport, just in case.' Abigail was on his passport and he said, 'Oh, Abigail is going to be stuck.' When I said, 'What are you talking about?' he replied, 'Never mind.' He wrote out a telephone number and an address and said, 'Here's the Kenyan address where we are supposed to be staying, just in case . . . ' I asked, 'Are you all right today?' He was very bright and singing. Normally I packed his bags, but that morning I didn't as I was unhappy that he was so pleased to be going without me. He packed a few things in his bag and when he was eating his breakfast he said, 'Caleb, will you pray for me that I can catch this plane today.' Caleb answered, 'I'm not going to pray.'

The Meakins family is well known to be late for everything! Andy left at 8.30 am for an 11.30 am takeoff. That was three hours! He started to go, then came back, and said he'd forgotten to kiss us! He was feeling so cheerful; he kissed us and left. I saw him smiling and happy as he drove off. Barry, his friend, came back with the car half an hour later.

I went to a meeting that day, followed by a wedding celebration, which I enjoyed. When I came home I said to the children, 'I'm tired today, we must go to bed.' We always had a time of devotion with the children and Lydia said, 'I hope Daddy's all right.' 'Why did you say that?' I asked. 'Of course he's all right.' But she said, 'I hope he is not killed.' I replied, 'Of course he's not.' Because Kenya is a place where there are many muggings and stabbings, I thought perhaps that was why she was afraid, so I said, 'Let's pray.'

I normally like to hear the news but that day we just went to bed at 8.00 pm. I don't normally go to sleep immediately but this time I did and was in a *deep* sleep. The phone rang and a girl I knew asked, 'Did Andy go to Kenya?' I said he did, to which she replied, 'What happened?' I answered, 'You've woken me up from a deep sleep.' 'OK,' she said, 'I'll see you tomorrow.' After that I couldn't get back to sleep. I started to worry. Why did she call me? She never called me. Why didn't I listen to the news? Why had I gone to sleep so early?

Ten minutes later there was a knock at my door. It was a girl who worked with me on the street girls' project. 'What's wrong?' I said. She replied, 'I have a problem; can I come in?' As soon as she said 'plane crash', I fainted.

We stayed up the whole night. Lydia woke up. 'I told you Daddy was killed.' I said, 'How do you know that?' 'I know, I know,' she said. I told her to go back to sleep, that Daddy was not necessarily dead; there were some survivors and he might be one of them. But there was no word from him and on Tuesday they told me that Andy was not among the survivors.

Fifty people survived out of 175. Andy was sitting next to an airhostess who survived and she accepted the Lord after the crash. She said, 'None of the passengers on that plane will go to hell because they were singing and praying in different languages and the atmosphere was very calm.' I asked a doctor who survived and he said, 'Even when the plane sank deep and we came up again, there was a quietness and a sense of God's presence.' The plane took off at 11.30 am and was hijacked some twenty minutes later.

It crashed around 4.00 pm so they were in the air all that time, but were not sure how serious the situation was. There was only about ten or fifteen minutes between the pilot saying they had run out of fuel, and the crash. I was told that Andy had known he was going to die and he was praying from Psalm 23 'Even though I walk through the valley of the shadow of death, I will fear no evil for you are with me.' Although Andy was in the valley of the shadow of death, he was still sharing the message with others. I knew he had compassion for people and he was a great man of prayer, but I didn't know he was still doing his work.

The week before Andy's death, when I went on the retreat, a lady was teaching us about being a widow. I felt this was *totally* irrelevant to me! However, God was preparing me for what was going to happen. She was telling us about her life story and I didn't know that it was for me!

Andy was loving and caring and was like a brother, a father, a husband to me, and my Christ model — I could see Christ shining out of him. Husbands and wives can be the closest friends and it can be seen from their walk together how God is working through them. Andy absolutely showed Christ to me and helped me to grow spiritually. When he died, I thought everything was finished. He was the one who reminded me to take my medicine, to rest, etc, and when I lost him I said, 'What am I going to do? Why God, has this happened? How am I going to live without him?' How am I going to bring up my children? Should they go to the Missionary school, which I can't afford to pay?' I went to my bedroom and searched through my Bible and God gave me two verses. One is Psalm 68:5, '[God] is a father to the fatherless, a defender of widows.'

Our plan had been to go to England in June the following year. We had a house near All Nations Bible College and I was going to join the Bible College; Andy had been undecided what he was going to do. But all our plans were turned upside down. I said, 'God, what am I going to do now?' The second verse he gave me was, 'Be still, and know that I am God.' I said, 'Thank you, Lord. You are the father to my children and you will defend me and guide me to what I should do. I am just going to depend on you.'

During a remembrance service, one of the airhostesses who survived said, 'Ruth, don't cry. Andy was witnessing in the plane to a friend of mine who didn't believe in God and they went to heaven together.' I immediately thought, 'If my husband was ministering on the plane, I should carry this on now.' I asked the missionaries if they would contact the wives of all those who died on the plane and invite them to join me in mourning. From that day, we started the Widows' Meeting and through it we reached two others who didn't know Christ and had lost their husbands. Our numbers grew and we prayed together at our monthly meetings.

This was *totally* irrelevant to me!

When we celebrated the first anniversary, we invited a preacher and we all shared our testimony of what God had done in our lives during that year — it was a real blessing, so something good came out of Andy's death.

Since then, God has been trying to teach me to depend on and completely trust in him. I know that before Andy went to catch his plane he was singing, 'Jehovah Jireh Lord Provider'. In Ethiopia when a partner dies, there is a court case and unless the case is finished it is not possible to get any money from the bank. When we lost Andy we phoned everywhere, Kenya, England, etc. I got the telephone bill and it was a lot of money. I was being hassled to pay it, but I didn't have that amount of money at that time, and my son was saying, 'Mummy, where's the money going to come from?' I told him, 'God will be in charge of that. He will pay, don't worry about it.'

I had never been in that position before; even as a child I never experienced shortage of money and now, with three children, I had nothing! That afternoon, two people came and gave me an envelope. When they had gone, I opened it and found the exact amount of money I needed for the telephone bill! I was absolutely shocked! I had heard from other people how God provided when they needed something, but I had never experienced this myself. I called Caleb and said, 'Look, I have all this money.' He asked, 'Who gave it?' and I told him that God gave it. He said, 'How come?' and I explained that these people had provided the exact amount, even though they had no idea how much I needed, but God knew and he sent them. He responded, 'Oh, they are very kind.'

Some people seemed to want me to mourn and complain about what God had done to me, and not give credit for what he had done *for* me. Perhaps I was depending too much on my husband without realising that he was human. I now depend on someone who is always there and will always be even through eternity! I say, 'Thank you, Lord. Yes, I'm a widow, but I am married to you now. I have you as my husband and I'm so grateful that you have time for me whenever I need you.' If I were a widow without Christ, how would I manage? It would be a disaster for my life and something I could not handle.

After Andy's death I decided not to move to England, but to stay in Ethiopia and see what God would do in my life. Andy's father died from cancer six months later, and I went to see his mum in the UK. I told her I thought I wouldn't be coming the next summer but I would let her know. Every time I visited England, Immigration stopped me and asked me different things; even when my husband was alive they gave me a hard time! The first time that no one stopped me was after Andy's death when I travelled for his Memorial Service.

We spoke with the British Embassy and they said that because I have three British children and I am Ethiopian, I needed a special paper to be able to come and go. I had to live in the UK for three years in order to get it, so, because of this and the difficulty in sorting out the children's schooling in Addis, I decided to live in England. I live next door to my sister-in-law, Andy's mum is only ten minutes walk from here, and the children's school is close as well. I'm now a full-time mum and looking after the children.

I don't know why I'm here but God has a purpose for me. Maybe I'll be a missionary in England, because I know most people here don't trust in Jesus. We used to have missionaries come from Britain to us. Now we need to come to England! I really enjoy witnessing, Andy used to say it was my gift. Someone once asked me, 'Why do you want to talk about Christ' and I replied, 'If I have something good, I like to share it with everybody. If you had a lot of money, wouldn't you want to share it with your family?' They said they would. What I have is more than money. It's life I want to share. I have a lot, and I want others to try it. I want them to share in what I have.'

When they had gone, I opened it . . .

PASTOR JACK HAYFORD
AN UNCOMMON TRUST AND FAVOUR

Because my parents moved a great deal during the depression years while my father was seeking work as a railroad switchman, we went to many different churches. Always the qualifying factor was, did the church preach the Word of God and the testimony of Christ as Saviour? The nearest church to our house that met those criteria was where we attended.

As a result of that I had exposure to a number of denominations in my upbringing. Looking back, I'm very grateful because it gave me a sense of appreciation for the larger Body of Christ and not just individual sectors. Furthermore, my parents, who were deeply committed and very biblically oriented in their values, and in the way they raised us children, were not bigoted — they were very non-legalistic. For example, we attended some churches that had extra-biblical requirements for holiness, certain do's and don'ts that were just standards of the local church and while my parents would never fight that, they never ensconced in us either a rebellion toward those attitudes nor an endorsement of them. So we grew up recognising that the love and life of Jesus Christ is something that is revealed in his Word and happens through his people in many different environments.

When I graduated to enter the ministry after four years' training at the Four Square School, my mother said, 'Well now, son, as you are launching out, you realise of course that no group has a corner on truth.' I said, 'Well, I know that, mama, but we, in our Pentecostal tradition, we're more right than anybody, aren't we?' She said, 'Son, I said it already — nobody has a corner on truth.' I really was rather taken aback, but I realised then, and thankfully it was early in my ministry, that every group feels they are more right than others.

While my parents never sacrificed their convictions, nor have I ever sacrificed mine, I was strongly influenced to recognise that being more right isn't the issue, ever. The issue is being more loving and understanding toward one another and just being grateful for the love of Jesus that we all share.

If there are doctrinal issues that anybody wants to discuss, then discuss, but don't debate. I believe that the spirit of debate is destructive because it pits competitively ideas against one another, and even if it's portrayed as trying to seek the truth, the bottom line of the truth is that it is incarnate in the person of Jesus. It is not in a set of doctrinal positions. Now, I'm no opponent of doctrine and I can make a doctrinal statement, but I think I've learnt enough to recognise that the real bottom line issues are the doctrine of who Jesus is — the Son of God — and how salvation is provided. We are called to live for him in the promise of his Word and not to use the Scriptures as an instrument for fighting. The Sword of the Spirit was not given for intramural warfare. It was given for doing battle against the adversary, the devil.

Not only is the church torn by dogma, and unnecessary infighting but the world is torn by cultural infighting and struggles that we usually put under the name of racial fighting, and although we talk about different races, the Bible never does. The Bible says there is one race — he has made of one blood all people who dwell on the face of the earth — it's one race, Adam's — and there are many ethnic groups within it that display God's unique creativity. To learn the value of those people in the uniqueness and distinction that each of them hold is, I think, a challenge for the church to provide leadership, not just in terms of Christian

I've learnt enough to recognise . . . the real bottom line

I always felt that I needed to wipe my hand!

generosity but in terms of modelling the Creator's will. What the Lord does in the church is redemption. What God has done in the world is creation. I think the church has to show something with regard to the Father's work in creation as surely as we are to show what Jesus has done in redemption. Building bridges of reconciliation is a primary call of the church, especially now at the turn of the Millennium.

Oakland had quite a significant black population, which affected me as a member of the dominant culture in America at that time. One of the things that the last twenty-five years has held for my life has been the discovery that despite being raised in a nation that was theoretically breaking down the laws of prejudice, there is still enormous capacity, not for hostility in my heart, but for *blindness* to the pain and the hurt of people in other cultures. We reinforce prejudice, as opposed to breaking it down, by jokes and by mocking one another. Although it's all supposed to be good fun, it really does wedge into place, however mild or apparently benign it may be, prejudice and separatism. In the long run it is very counter-productive, if not destructive. It is everywhere in humanity.

The church likes to think that it's above it. In different ways, unperceived separatism, either within the church or within the culture, impacts our life and thought more than we recognise. Early in my ministry I was serving in a small church in Indiana that my wife and I had planted. One afternoon while building some shelves for Sunday School I was listening to the radio. A commentator said that, in the light of a particular civil rights struggle back in the late fifties and early sixties, 'It is impossible to have been raised in 20th century America and not be prejudiced, racially.' I thought to myself, 'That's not true.' I thought of my home town, and said to myself, 'I'm not prejudiced.' The instant I said that, it was as though God turned on a video player in my mind and I saw something about myself that no one had ever taught me. I was raised by parents who had not devalued anybody, but what I saw was due to the *impact of the culture.* God showed me a picture of myself shaking hands with a black person and when I withdrew from the handshake, while I didn't do it, I always felt that I needed to wipe my hand! It was a profound self-discovery and I wept, because I didn't know that this was in me.

That was the beginning of a pilgrimage and I became more aware of the impact of the culture on me. I've often said that, in a sense, I understand some of this too because much of my life has been spent as a Pentecostal preacher. Entering the Pentecostal ministry in the late 1950s, there was far more prejudice against Pentecostalism in the Christian church than there is today.

I came to understand what it meant to be ostracised by the dominant part of the culture so that, in a sense, I grew up as a victim of prejudice. I never thought of myself that way but I realised years later, that in fact I did respond in some environments with a sense of being inferior. I felt it necessary to verify my worth, when in fact I loved Christ just as dearly as anyone else did but was treated as a *tolerated* part of the community, as opposed to a *welcomed* part. When I understood that, I began to realise how many sectors of the church I viewed in the same way.

I think it takes the Spirit of God to reveal this in us because I don't think it is something most people do consciously. Most people, especially believers in Christ, don't calculate being unloving, but we have been acculturated with less love. Much separatism in the Body of Christ is not only unperceived, but in many cases the separatism is reinforced as a value — that's one of the means by which superior righteousness is verified. I believe the Holy Spirit is working in a great way in the church across the face of the world right now, removing those things.

I don't think the Holy Spirit wants to precipitate an undiscerning unity that reduces things to the lowest common denominator but rather to gather us around the highest common denominator, the Lord Jesus himself. If we gather around him, the cross and the Scriptures, and magnify the Saviour, these other things though not unimportant, are not important enough to keep us apart.

From my earliest recollection I understood the way of the Lord. My parents say that there was an instance when I was five years old when I came home from Sunday School and said that I'd asked Jesus into my heart. I don't recall this, but it does indicate that there was a general recognition of the need to do that. What I remember more clearly is when I was eight years old and there was an invitation to open our hearts to Christ, I consciously resisted it. I resisted it because I thought that my friends would make fun of me.

It became very clear in my heart that no matter what my disposition was in general towards the Lord, I was also a sinner who was resistant to God and that he was more interested in me than I was in him and his will and way.

When I was ten years old I made a very conscious, open declaration to receive Christ as Saviour, responding to an evangelistic invitation on Sunday night, 25th February 1945. I can remember it very clearly. I remember going home knowing that the Spirit of God had done a work in my heart. There was a tremendous feeling of joy. A ten-year-old little boy could not conjure that up by himself. No-one talked me into that. I *knew* that I had entered into a relationship with the Lord.

Prior to that, I was aware from as long as I can remember, not only that I needed the Lord but of the sense that I was supposed to be in public ministry. I did everything I could to try and talk myself into something else, because I had other interests. In fact, I would bargain with God. I knew I should help people, so I thought, 'Well, I'll be a doctor!' But I couldn't do that because I just shuddered at the sight of blood. I finally decided that I would be a pharmacist, but when I was sixteen I went to a Presbyterian Youth Rally and when there was a call to give everything to Christ, I went forward and committed myself to full-time ministry.

About a year later while attending a vibrant Christian Missionary Alliance in the Oakland area I thought, 'I'll go to their Bible College.' Two months before I graduated from High School, a relatively unknown Pentecostal evangelist by the name of Oral Roberts came to town for some meetings, and for the first time I saw a non-fanatical Pentecostalism. There were genuine instances of people being touched by the power of God, and his ministry impacted me with solidity. He preached the Bible, glorified Jesus, and large numbers of people came to Christ. I knew that the commitment I'd made to ministry had to be focused in that direction so I changed my plans and went to Life Bible College.

Not until after that happened and I made that commitment, did my parents tell me that, when I was a one-year-old infant they had brought me for dedication to the Lord. Watson Teaford, the pastor who prayed for me, said later that he had felt impressed not to just pray, 'Lord, have your purpose in this child's life' but specifically 'Lord, take this child and use him for the ministry.' Seventeen years later when I went to Bible College to study, he was the Dean of the College and had a great influence on my life.

I met my attractive wife Anna while we were in college. She was raised in Nebraska and I was drawn to her not only because of her obvious commitment to Christ, but also by the simple genuineness of this Nebraska girl. She was intelligent — an Honours student — and I am thankful to this day that everybody who knows my wife says that what you see is what you get.

When we left college to go into ministry, we were very young and involved in youth work.

I just shuddered at the sight of blood

We planted the church in Indiana and four years later, in 1960, I was asked to become the National Youth Director for the Four Square Church in Los Angeles. I served in that office for five years and then returned to the Life Bible College as the Dean of Students. During that time the Lord blessed our enterprise and we had a great deal to do with the growth of the college. It appeared that my direction would be in Christian Higher Education but in my fifth year I knew the Lord was redirecting my paths. Anticipating that at the end of the school year we would return to the Pastorate, we agreed to help a small church called The Church on The Way in the San Fernando Valley. It was without a pastor and only had eighteen members. We would help at weekends.

In the ensuing year God showed, without any doubt, that he wanted me to stay there. It was a small congregation, little building, nothing about it suggesting much promise! But the impression he gave me was so profound that I knew I couldn't escape it. I didn't want to do it but I stayed because I feared God was going to ruin my life if I didn't! About that same time the Lord began to deal with me about the priority of worship in the life of the church, and things just began to fall into place. With my understanding of how that priority could be applied in the life of a congregation, we began to lead our congregation this way, with a continued focus on the Word and a love for people.

There came, in 1971, a visitation of the Spirit of God to the church — a real disclosure of the glory of God. Jesus said to the Father, in John Chapter 17, 'Father, I have given them the glory that you gave me,' and it was as though we *literally* were given a gift of a visitation of God's glory. It was the first Saturday of 1971, 4.30 in the afternoon, and I had been at the church all day, studying in my office. Before going home I walked through the sanctuary to set the thermostat by the platform so that the church would be warm the next day — it was very chilly in January. I turned around and found the room was filled with a visible silvery mist. I just stood there, stunned by it, looking around to see if there was a natural explanation for it. I was really bewildered. I went into the prayer room to see if there was anything like it in there. There wasn't. So I rubbed my eyes, returned to the sanctuary and found it still the same. I stood there, thinking to myself, 'I wonder if this is what people see when they see the glory of God?' And a voice spoke to me. It was an internal voice — not like a sound in the room — and the first thing the voice said was, 'It's what you think it is!' And then the Lord said, 'I've given my glory to dwell in this place.' I stood there, thinking. I hadn't been on an extended fast or anything like that. It wasn't anything that I'd even asked for, in fact I thought, in my mind, that God didn't give his glory to anybody. *I thought that thought*!

As I watched it gradually disappeared, and was gone. *But I knew that it wasn't gone*. I was so taken aback — you would think a really spiritual person would have got onto their knees and praised God or something! I was so disarmed by it that I just stood there and thought to myself, 'Praise God.' I went home and looked in the Bible where it says, 'I will not give my glory to another' and found it's talking about the heathen deities. Jesus said, in John Chapter 17, 'Father, I've given them the glory that you gave me,' and in Ephesians it says, 'to him be glory in the Church and in Christ Jesus'. I told two or three people about my experience in the next couple of weeks, but didn't talk about it publicly for over two years.

The next day, instead of the usual 100 or 110 in church, there were 170 — the next day! The church began to grow and by the end of the year it was 350 and the year after that, it was 700. There was no human explanation for what happened. It just came as a surge. The church today has about 10,000 members, a weekly attendance of between 6,000 and 7,000 and around 75,000 people have received Christ.

**The first thing
the voice
said was . . .**

The Lord called us to stay there, and the church now occupies 24 acres. To relocate and build on the edge of town would have been far more convenient and far more impressive, but we were explicitly directed by the Spirit of God, through our elders praying together, to stay. That seemed a real disadvantage to us, because when we began, we only had two-thirds of an acre and a tiny little building. You couldn't buy plots of land so we would just buy a piece here and a piece there. Then, ten years ago, there was a relocation of the First Baptist Church of Van Nuys and we were able to buy another complete campus, with eight major buildings and ten acres of property, only one and a half miles from the campus we already had. We kept our original campus development, so we now have what we call the East and West Campus.

The numeric attendance of the church today really isn't the most important part of its influence, many different things have happened through the outreach of the church. Over a hundred churches have been born out of our church. They have a four-year College and we have a three-year Seminary — the King's College and the King's Seminary. There are many missionaries, in addition to radio and television broadcasts, writing and music, and God has given us a voice in the city of Los Angeles. It has been a great privilege to serve in one inner city church of this size for so long, and to have a chance genuinely to impact one of the world's major cities.

God has given me uncommon favour and trust with pastors from other denominations and there's no way that could be earned or bought. The recognition of our church around the world is amazing. You could not make that happen, nor the widespread use of my song 'Majesty'. The Lord has done things that are just amazing to me.

Anna and I have four children — two boys and two girls, and many grandchildren. Our daughter, Rebecca, is an award-winning writer and married to Scott who is my right-hand person and the heir apparent to the pulpit of the church. This is at the will of our elders — in our structure we could not manipulate this, and on our principles we would not. Our son, Jack, works as a chemist in the paper industry, our other son, Mark, is in the computer business and our youngest daughter, Christa, is married to a very gifted young pastor. So we have a wonderful family, all committed to the Lord and doing well.

Anna spends most of her time helping me service the demands of our life. She is constantly sought after by women in our church because of her stability and proven practical wisdom. She does considerable counselling and encouraging, is regularly asked to write for journals and also chapters in books for pastors' wives. If you asked Anna what her ministry is, she'd say, 'Well, just to love the people and to help Jack.' The story of my life is largely influenced by the impact of my parents, the impact of my wife and of course, most of all, the impact of the Lord Jesus.

The centrepiece of my personal life is just spending time with the Lord. Jesus is not only my Saviour and Lord, but I *know* that Jesus intimately loves *me*, that he calls me by name. I believe the primary objective of the Father is that he sees such an intrinsic value in every individual that he created, that he doesn't want it to be lost. Jesus is the instrument, the Saviour who has come, not just to save people from their sins, but to rescue and restore that value in each person and to see it recovered, reinstated and fully realised. When that happens, it's the highest fulfilment that a created being can know, but it takes a Redeemer to make it happen. Jesus is that Redeemer.

When that happens, it's the highest fulfilment

SAMI DAGHER
LIVING BEYOND THE LIMITS

I am the youngest in a family of twelve, and because my mother was really tired she didn't want me. She tried everything possible to get rid of me but it didn't work! She boiled herbs and drank them because she was told this would terminate the pregnancy but it seemed God wanted me to be born.

My father was a farmer although it was only planting wheat with a couple of cows in the old fashioned way. When he discovered that farming was not sufficient to feed the family, he started building. He began to make a little more money than in farming and decided to buy land. My mother used to help him sell eggs, cheese and yoghurt to the neighbours in the village and whenever they had saved sufficient money, they would buy more land. I went to school, but in the afternoons I used to go to the fields and help with the cows. I was a little devil when I was young and didn't really want to study!

My father tried to make a man out of me; he wanted me to go to the best schools and was ready to sell his land to send me to university, but I was no good at school. I eventually went to an hotelier school in Beirut to study management, graduating three years later, after which I went to train and work in Switzerland. I wanted to work in hotels all over the world and then start my own international hotel in Lebanon, so I spent seven years living in France, England, Turkey, Libya and Italy. My last post was in England. While working in a hotel in Blackpool I met Joy who was working there as a receptionist. We soon decided to get married in London and then moved to Lebanon. I will never forget the tears on her face as she looked over to the small hills of England from the top deck of the ship. I was uprooting a girl from her family and she had never even been out of her country.

Do we have to start discussing things like this?

My first job was in cabaret, but I left that to work at the Intercontinental Hotel. I was searching for true happiness and the meaning of life and hadn't been able to find it in drink, travelling or women. Deep down in my heart there were questions: why are we here? What is real happiness? I enjoyed life, drinking and dancing, but real joy, everlasting joy, was missing. My parents-in-law left England and were planning to make their home with us. They brought with them a religious magazine and as I was reading it, the name Jesus attracted me.

In 1967 when the Israelis attacked, during the Six Day War, the British Embassy advised all British subjects to return to England so my parents-in-law went back. The magazine stayed however, and made a great impression on me, because I really wanted to learn more about Jesus. One day, sitting with an artist who worked in the Casino of Lebanon, we were discussing questions about religion, which really upset her. She said, 'Is this the right time — we are having a drink — do we have to start discussing things like this?' She then delved into her bag and fished out a card saying, 'I was in a shopping precinct today and a couple of American missionaries came to the shop. They began talking to me and witnessing about Christ and they gave me this card. Phone them, and they'll answer you!' I went home and said to Joy, 'Phone them!' We agreed to meet them on my day off but that day the General Manager of the hotel rang to say, 'There is a big party and you've got to be here,' so I said to Joy, 'You go!'

When I came home I asked her, 'How was your day? Tell me about your meeting with those people,' to which she replied, 'Oh, they are nice, but all they talk about is Jesus, Jesus, Jesus.' I asked if they said good or bad things about him. She responded, 'Oh, good things, but they

I didn't dare tell him what had happened

talk far too much about Jesus.' I arranged to meet them and we started a Bible study together. For six months I studied and argued with them until one afternoon they asked me, 'Would you like to accept Jesus as your personal Saviour?' Joy was one hundred percent ready and understood what she was doing. With me, it was fanaticism. What, do you think Jesus is only for you? He is for me too! Of *course*, I want to accept him! So we knelt down together and prayed for salvation. But deep in my heart I was thinking, 'This is good for my wife. Now she won't keep on at me, asking me where I've been, why I'm late, or why . . . So, it's good. Let her accept Christ.' And really, that's what happened.

I used to finish work every night at midnight, get drunk and arrive home at four in the morning. Eventually there was no more excitement and when I went home there was no companionship. Joy had stopped drinking, she stopped smoking, and she stopped fighting. I wanted somebody to fight with me! She wouldn't fight any more! It was awful. I began hurting her with words and action, so she rang the missionaries and said, 'Sami is having a battle. You have to come and pray with me and you need to talk to him.' They came and we talked and it certainly was a battle. We argued and fought together because I was angry with Joy for sharing our secrets with other people, but it was decision time — yes or no to Jesus. It was a crossroads. We finally prayed together and relaxed, but I still did not make that *real commitment*.

One week, with business slow due to the Arab-Israeli war — tourists were not coming to Lebanon — I was wandering up and down in the restaurant and I now know what I heard was the Holy Spirit talking to my heart. He said, 'If you were a communist, what would you say, Long live America, or Long live Russia?' I thought: 'A Communist would say, Long live Russia, not America!' He continued, 'OK, you are a Christian, but by your life and actions, you are saying, Long live Satan, not Christ. Why don't you change your religion, become a Muslim, a Jew, become whatever you wish? If you *are* a Christian, you know from studying the Bible how you should live, and if you don't want to live that way, change your religion.' The name of Christ drew me but I was so weak I could not live up to the demands. I continued rejecting what the Spirit was saying to me but the thoughts would not leave me. Eventually at about ten o'clock that night I walked into the swimming pool area, nobody was there. I knelt down behind a big column, and said, 'Lord, forgive me. I am a sinner. Please not only forgive me, but also give me strength to live for you tonight. Only tonight.'

At midnight the bartender sent a boy with a message to me saying, 'Your drink is ready for you. What are you doing? We are all here so come and join us.' I told the boy to go back and say I was busy. The bartender knew I wasn't because there was no business, so he came along to find me and asked, 'What are you doing? We are waiting for you!' I said, 'I don't want a drink tonight!' He responded, 'What do you mean? We've got it all arranged. We've got so and so with us and we're going to such and such a place.' I replied, 'I'm busy tonight. I'm not going anywhere.' I didn't dare tell him what had happened but I had decided not to go out with them. I took a taxi straight home. Joy was asleep in bed, so I went into the lounge, knelt down and prayed, 'Lord, thank you for giving me this strength.' I don't remember how long I prayed and read for, but eventually I went to sleep. In the morning when I wakened, I felt so free and light. It was as if a heavy load had been rolled off my shoulders. Joy brought me coffee and there was a packet of cigarettes but I didn't smoke them. I used to smoke three packets a day so when people offered me a cigarette and I refused they asked, 'What is the matter with you?' For three days, I couldn't tell anyone, but eventually I could not put it off any longer and I told them that I had accepted Christ. I suffered quite a bit of persecution from my friends and it was a big temptation to renege but God held me by his grace. For one whole month, each day I prayed, 'Just today, Lord, only today' and then at the end of the month I said, 'Lord, my whole life is yours.' By the grace of God I am where I am now, still living for him.

In 1971 I went to a conference in Amsterdam where Dr Billy Graham preached about the need for people to serve God in Europe, the Middle East and Africa. In his closing message he said, 'If God has spoken to you this week, just pray in your own language and promise God something.' There were about 4,000 of us and I stood in that huge auditorium and prayed aloud in Arabic saying, 'Lord, I want to serve you.' It was an inspirational moment with everyone praying in his own language.

Business picked up and we had the best years in the Lebanon for tourists because Egypt and Israel had signed the peace agreement. The hotel was one hundred percent full all the time and I was making a lot of money. I forgot my promise to God but whenever I went to church, instead of blessing me, God was rebuking me.

One day when the pastor of the International Church was away in Jordan, his wife asked someone else to come and preach. This man's message was: 'God is looking for someone — he needs someone!' I was critical of this preacher, disagreeing with his theology. 'How can he say, "God needs". If he is God, he doesn't need anyone! God is God.' At home I was following the advice of a friend who said, 'Read from the Old Testament, the Psalms, Proverbs and the New Testament every day.' I was reading in the New Testament where Jesus entered Jerusalem from the Mount of Olives. He told his disciples they would find a donkey in the village, to untie it and if asked what they were doing, to say that the Lord had need of it! Suddenly I was brought up short. It was really a message from the Holy Spirit. He said, 'If the Lord needs a donkey, He needs you! So there is no more excuse. He *needs* you!'

Suddenly I was brought up short

However, I found another excuse to put before the Lord. I said, 'Lord, all the people I met in Amsterdam had titles — Professor so-and-so, Doctor so-and-so, Reverend so-and-so. I have *nothing*. I am only a table servant. You can't choose someone who is nothing.' I felt confident that I had convinced him!

Once again, when the pastor was away from our church we had a visitor from England to preach. He read the story of David and Saul and how they put the armour on David to go and fight Goliath. No sooner had he read the passage than it seemed the Holy Spirit opened my ears and began speaking to me personally. He said, 'You see, the armour of Saul was too big for David. He took only a couple of stones and he killed the enemy using his sling. Go you likewise and use what you have, and God will kill the enemy through you.' I was one hundred percent convinced that was the voice of the Holy Spirit in me.

I went home and told Joy, 'We are going to take a three-day holiday up in the mountains. We are going to take the children with us and I want to spend it in fasting and prayer because we have a great decision to make.' She agreed, and so we went up into the mountains and fasted the first day. I couldn't keep the news from Joy and so I told her that I was going to resign my job and wanted to serve the Lord full-time. It was in 1973. The two years of fighting with God were over! Joy was a tremendous help and said, 'Sami, if you bring a dry loaf of bread to me when you are serving the Lord, it's better than all the money that you are making at the Intercontinental Hotel.'

After I left my job at the hotel I went to a Baptist Bible School in Beirut. I wanted to see what they taught and thought perhaps I could learn more about the Bible and about the Lord Jesus. After two months I realised it was really a waste of time because it was going to take me three years, and I knew the Lord had called me to go and serve, not to go and be at school!

In 1975 the war started. All the missionaries left and we had no food, nothing, so Joy went out to teach in a school and I began cooking and washing the dishes. One day I prayed, 'Lord, if you don't provide for me, I'm going to go back to work.' That week, the Lord provided a sum of money, which was three times more than my wife's wage. I asked her to resign and since then God has taken care of us.

I stayed in my home for three months, just reading, praying, watching the bullets, rockets, and fighting from our window. Then the Lord led me to start home Bible studies. One man who accepted the Lord through these studies had a building and he told me, 'Go to the Karantina, I have a building down there. I'll give you two rooms. They are burned. Go and start a church there. Start a ministry!'

Now the Karantina is the dirtiest place in the whole of Lebanon. It's the rubbish dump of the city of Beirut. Refugees from Kurdistan and Palestine inhabited it. It was an awful place.

During that time there were a couple of months of peace, so the missionaries returned. I told them what I was going to do and one wife said, 'Well, Sami, if I were you, I would not go down there. I'd find another place.' We had prayed about it and I felt a real peace so I said that the Lord was leading down there, and what could I do? We fixed the two rooms, bought benches, and then we started a church with perhaps three or four people.

There was shelling and bombing everywhere

The man gave us a prayer room — we call it the prayer room because we used to meet up there to pray every Sunday. For two or three months there was no preaching, no message, nothing, just reading the Word of God, prayer and fasting. At Christmas 1976 we had the first meeting in the two rooms. After the first year the place was full with about fifty people and we were forced to enlarge the church. During the war, this happened four times and even though there was shelling and bombing everywhere, people were coming to hear the Word of God.

When I began the ministry it was very difficult. I didn't know the Bible very well and it used to take me a week to prepare a message because I wanted to be doctrinally correct. I wanted to honour Christ and to build up the people. The Holy Spirit led me. He said, 'If you really want to make a church, you have to read the Acts of the Apostles and see how the first church was built.' I read and reread the Book of Acts and tried to build a church just like that first one.

Because of the agony I went through the Lord led me to start a Bible School. I want to teach the whole Bible because there is so *much* false teaching around now, where people take one verse and make a doctrine out of it. I believe we have to teach the *whole* Bible. We don't teach doctrine, we teach the Word of God and this is how God has blessed us.

When on many Sundays we had to close the church because of the war, I would go and visit people in their homes. They were living in shelters, under steps, anywhere, and I used to pray with them, read with them, encourage them and then return home. Often Joy asked me not to go because she did not want to become a widow in a foreign country. I used to comfort her and tell her that nothing would happen to me. Only people like Paul and Peter were worthy to die for the name of Christ. I said, 'I'm not worthy. He will never give me that honour.' She used to relax a bit then!

I can remember one day when there was no bread anywhere. An acquaintance who belongs to a political party was allowed to go through the green lines so I told him we needed bread and he said he could bring us some. He went about forty kilometres from my home, crossing the green line between the Lebanese and Muslim forces and bought about 100 packets of bread, each holding about ten loaves, so I was able to supply the neighbours and the church members, when I could get to them.

I am on the Executive Committee of an orphanage in the mountains and I was sure they needed bread so I said to Joy, 'You stay here. I have to drive to the orphanage to give them the bread.' She was angry and begged me not to go. 'Can't you hear the bombing?' It was like rain. Rockets were falling everywhere. I replied, 'Joy, the Lord has told me. I have to go. You stay down in the shelter where you are safe and don't worry about me.'

I drove up into the mountains, and the Lord is my witness, there was a rocket at the left side, and one at the right. Parts of the mountain were burning all around. Houses were destroyed. There was smoke everywhere, there was one car only on the road, and that was mine!

When I got to the orphanage and gave them the bread, the lady whom we call 'Mother' said, 'We ate the last loaf of bread last night and I told the boys, "We have no more food. You have to pray to Jesus that he will bring you food." And this is the answer to the boys' prayer.' So I gave them the forty packets of bread and drove back safely, through the same terrible conditions, to my home and family.

In spite of the shelling and bombing, we have tried to live a normal life. We even went camping for twenty days in the mountains with our children. I took my son Paul outside to lie on the floor and watch the tracers going by. Joy used to sit inside shouting, 'Come in, come in!'

Our home in Ashruferu was on the 6th floor, up in the roof. One night an announcement came over the loudspeakers, 'The enemy is using rockets that will destroy the top two floors so be sure not to sleep in an apartment under the roof.' We went down two floors to a place near the steps, where it was open. An anti-aircraft bullet came from West Beirut and it hit the steps and came down. Our daughter Anna was sleeping there and it went through her pyjama jacket and then her pyjama trousers and burned the mattress underneath. We kept that bullet and gave it to her on her wedding day, as a reminder of the goodness of God who protected her. She would have been killed otherwise.

On another occasion I was praying with Joy for a family who lived near Hotel Dieu, as we heard on the news that that area had been shelled. When the shelling started near us we went down into the shelter. We were still listening to the news that massive shelling was continuing near Hotel Dieu. I cannot say I heard a voice, but the thought came to me: 'Why are you praying for them? Why don't you go and get them and bring them here. It's much safer.' They are a large family with the father, the mother, and four children. I turned to Joy, 'This is what the Lord is saying. I am going to fetch them from Hotel Dieu and bring them here.' She thought I was crazy and honestly, it was a crazy act. But if you don't live beyond the limits you cannot experience God's protection and his work! So I convinced her to remain in the shelter, and because of the size of the family, I took the van, which is large and more likely to be hit than a small car. I went to the shelter where they were living at the bottom of their building behind sandbags. They couldn't believe that I was there to collect them. They didn't dare move. I begged them to come with me and they wouldn't move! I said, 'OK, what can I do for you?' The mother said they had no money or bread. They had nothing, and could I get them something to eat. I answered, 'If I give you money, is there somewhere here you can buy things?' They said there were shops so I gave them money.

The shelling was what they call the 'Stellings' Organ' — sixty rockets going off at one time and spreading all over an area. There was about five or ten minutes respite during the time it was being reloaded. We got used to it. They had just launched a full attack and then it stopped. So I told the family I had just five or ten minutes to leave and they were very concerned. But I insisted. I drove the van like mad. There was nobody else on the street. I'd just got to a bridge, when the shelling started again. If I had remained with the family down in the shelter I would

I begged them to come with me . . .

have been safe, but if I had left the van in front of their building, it would have been shelled because the rockets arrived in exactly the position in which it had been parked. To Joy's great relief I got home safely.

Our plans for the future are to preach the gospel among the 200 million Arabic speaking people. We want to reach our own people and that's our responsibility. We know the language and we feel that witnessing for Christ is not an option. It's a *must*. Paul said, 'Woe to me if I do not preach the gospel [of Christ].' That is why we were not satisfied with Lebanon only. I have sent missionaries to Iraq, Africa and Syria and I know it is dangerous work, but our God is a mighty God and he can make a way where there is no way.

The Lord gave me a vision to send a tent-maker to start a church in Baghdad. The war came and spoiled the vision but after the ceasefire in 1991 the Lord spoke to me again so I went. I took relief and medicines and we gave out 40,000 New Testaments in the streets of Baghdad.

We have purchased a piece of land there and, God willing, I will be taking an architect to design a church, and then we will start building. In Iraq, it's forbidden by law to meet in homes because a home is not considered a worship place and people meeting like that are considered a sect. There is freedom for religion but a church building is required to be able to worship.

The Bible Society has opened a shop in Baghdad and there is a great hunger for the gospel of Christ. It's a very difficult job because they believe that America, England and France are Christian countries and they say, 'Look what the Christian countries have done to us.' It is our job to show them the love of Christ so that they can see it is politics and not Christian countries, that has done this to them. I sent a letter to Sadam Hussein concerning this and the letter was published in all the newspapers of Iraq. He also gave an order that the film *Jesus* should be shown on national TV and twenty million people saw that film.

We know that our battle is against principalities and powers of the evil one. We know our only weapon is prayer. This is why the Holy Spirit laid it on my heart to begin the prayer room in the Karantina. The Lord Jesus said to pray without ceasing. This prayer room is open twenty-four hours a day; even during the war when we were absent, it was never closed. *Never closed*. People from this area could come, push the door open, come inside, and pray. I really believe this is the secret of the power, of the blessing, of the Lord in our church. It's the prayer in that room.

We believe that the Karantina Church is one of the Lord's miracles, because it is the fastest growing church in the *known* history of the Middle East. Perhaps when Peter was preaching, there were 5,000 coming in one day! But since missionaries have been coming to the Middle East, this is the fastest growing church.

It is very hard because we are dealing with fanatical Catholics and Muslims. If a person from a Catholic background becomes a Protestant, they are accused of selling out their religion and if the background is Muslim, that person can be killed by their own family. So this is why, if only one person a year is won for Christ here, it is marvellous. When someone declares that they are a believer here, they *must be a real believer*, because it is so costly.

. . . that person can be killed by their own family

I was born in Bombay and have two sisters and four brothers. My father was a medical doctor and had become the head of a multinational pharmaceutical company. He was a very busy man but always made sure he had special time for each of us. We had a very high lifestyle and were all geared towards going to the best universities in the world and never looking back.

When I was fifteen years old my father died following a heart attack. This was a big shock to me; it shattered my cocooned life existence. I started to wonder about God, about human beings, about life, and quite early on I became an atheist.

At the age of sixteen, as I joined college, I became a Marxist and at the same time got into drugs. I found the whole experience of drugs so pleasurable and it helped me to forget my father's death. I started to use them quite erratically, spent a lot of money and did not do much else with my life.

Quite soon I became addicted and in an economic mess, unable to continue with my college education. I decided to try and renounce the world so I started living in the Himalayas. I managed quite well in the mountains except that I was still unable to cope with the basic grief of my father's death. My life didn't seem to mean anything, whether it was up in the mountains or in the middle of the city, so what I had gone to seek I was unable to find.

I came through Delhi in the middle of a drugs run, carrying a few kilos of hashish, on my way to Goa where it would sell for a very high price. For some reason I got stuck in Delhi and met a missionary from Northern Ireland who asked me if I wanted help. I was surprised at the genuineness with which he asked this question, so I replied 'Yes, I really do want help. I feel I'm at the end of the road. I'm living up in the Himalayas and can't seem to find any answers to the questions that I have. I'm doing something I don't want to be doing. I never wanted to be dealing in hash, I'd be much happier trying to find what life means up in the mountains.'

He directed me to a Christian Community called Ashiana, meaning 'nest', and I stayed there for a little while. They weren't able to cope with me and I wasn't able to cope with them so I went on to Goa and other places. But I was touched by the care and the love in this community, and so much to their initial dismay, I think, I came back.

One day while doing a Bible study with them from the first letter of John I came across the verse which says, 'If any one says "I love God," yet hates his brother, he is a liar.' What a powerful statement. I realised I had a lot of hatred and anger in me and this was definitely blocking my discovery of God's love or being able to experience that in a full way. I stopped using drugs, and as I read more and more in the Bible studies, I discovered Jesus' teaching about prayer in Matthew Chapter 6. He talked about going into a private room and not doing something in public, so I went into a room, locked the door and prayed to Christ, saying 'If you can change my life, I'm ready. Please do it.'

While I slept I had a vision of Christ with scales on which were good and bad, and the bad seemed to be weighing right down to the floor. The message I received was 'Luke, I want to see the scales tip to the other side.' I woke up full of the Holy Spirit. I felt that I was cleaned out inside and had an overwhelming sense of joy.

I was surprised at the genuineness

When a call came from a local evangelical church to start a care programme in a slum, our community responded, and although I was such a young Christian, I became elected leader of the programme.

I wanted to support myself, not to be dependent on other people, so I found a part-time job. The rest of the time I did Bible studies and worked in the slum with a young woman, Meera, who was on a research programme but had also come to the Ashiana community to sort out her life. After a year we both began praying as to whether or not we should do this work full time. During that same month five children died of malnutrition and we felt that was a sign for us to say to God, 'OK, whatever you're doing, this is where your calling is.' We both relinquished all the other work we were involved in and started a full-time programme in the slum that later became the organisation we called Sharan.

I married Meera, and as we wanted to share God's love with the poor in a qualitative way, we worked with one community and looked at the various different needs. We saw that the whole process of structural injustice was so strong that a huge amount of work was needed. We began income generation programmes and started a community health programme, with Kiran Martin as our first full-time doctor.

Can't you wash her face at least?

The next six or seven years were a very intense phase in my life; I had become angry at the injustices people had faced and the laissez-faire attitude of the government and the different institutions that were supposed to be providing services and support, which were just not forthcoming. As I worked in the slums I understood more and more what conditions people lived in and the way they were treated. We could wait for an hour to see a doctor in a government hospital, for a child who was really sick with chronic diarrhoea or something like that and who had lost 5 kg of body weight. A young doctor, barely qualified, would shout at the woman, 'How dare you bring this child to see me like this? Can't you wash her face at least? Can't you keep the child clean? How do you expect a child to be OK?'

We knew from being in the slum that they would have to walk 1 km to get water and then often, when opening the taps of the houses where they could get water, dogs would come and bite them. They would have to steal the water and bring it on their heads in pots just to survive. He had no *clue* about the conditions in which these people lived and the assumption was that they were lazy, ignorant, and dirty, hence their condition. It really made me angry and it kept happening and happening and happening. Quite often I erupted! I really yelled at the doctors and people in the different government offices. I wasn't at peace and it was affecting my work, leadership and faith. I realised that cumulatively it actually had led to burnout and I needed to take some time off to come to terms with that.

I went to All Nations Christian College in Hertfordshire, England, and did a course in Mission. I also did a Cambridge degree in Theology that helped me delve further into questions that I was asking. All Nations had an emphasis on worship and prayer as part of the programme whereas in the Theology degree even the existence of God could not be presumed without some supportive academic evidence. The questions helped me reconcile some doubts about my faith. I had learned about Christ in an experiential way and while doing Bible studies, but when one put the Bible to the test and realised the width and depth with which it has been studied, it became a living faith, but a living faith in a historical context. I learned that they actually *found* the pool at Bethesda historically, through John's narrative, and not through other historical texts. That, for me, was reinforcement and helped to strengthen my belief, especially since one got to research processes that enabled us to say that our faith is not completely anecdotal but is historically verifiable and there are markers for it right through history.

The time off allowed me to work through some of my doubts and thoughts, like when you pray for a child and the child dies. Why couldn't this child have been brought to life? And then you see the parents grieve and have to come to terms with that. When I left for England I'd seen so many deaths I just did not want to see another one — I couldn't cope with it any more — so in a sense while I was studying there was also a healing process taking place.

With our studies completed we returned to Sharan, to be faced with a huge drug problem in the slums. Because of my own experience with drugs, and that of a few people who had also given up drugs while working with me, we felt we were in the best position to do something. Initially people were just inhaling heroin but there was a rapid shift to injecting, so we commenced treatment programmes for their addiction and HIV.

Our approach in dealing with HIV is modelled on the way Jesus dealt with leprosy. He didn't ask too many questions, he just put his hands out, provided care and God's love. Something significant, which I will always keep with me, is that when Jesus healed the ten lepers only one came back to praise him. He asked where the other nine were. But the fact is, healing went out to all ten!

We don't ask that all those we care for become Christians, but we do want them to know that this is an experience of God's love. We have also been doing pioneering work without trying to capitalise on it or create too much media attention. I think that has been respected not only by what we call the bilateral and multilateral agencies and the big donor agencies, but also the Christian donor agencies and the HIV positive group. We started a Continuum of Care, which involves the government, voluntary agencies, and some of the Christian service agencies, in a network that provides comprehensive care from the hospital right down to the home. We have programmes across the city of Delhi and where we didn't seek to receive as much as to give, the networking was much more successful. I think this is partly why the World Health Organisation has identified us as a role model.

Something that has always stayed with me as one of our mission statements is a comment from Mother Teresa; she said that 'we are not social workers but contemplatives in the heart of the world'. That is exactly what I believe we should be — we should be reflecting on the issues around us — issues of justice, issues of poverty, issues of need, issues of marginalisation, and most of all we need to see how God would have us respond to that.

Our approach in dealing with HIV is . . .

BARONESS CAROLINE COX
A VOICE FOR THE VOICELESS

I came into this world on 6th July 1937, born in Highgate, North London. My father was a Consultant Surgeon and my mother, a qualified teacher, but living as a full-time wife and mother. We were evacuated down to Devon in the early years of the war and my earliest memory is riding my little tricycle, looking up, and seeing the puffballs — presumably anti-aircraft — in the sky. Towards the end of the war when I was six or seven, there was the phenomenon of the doodlebug and the great fear when the engines cut out. As long as the engines were still running they were moving but once they stopped they immediately exploded. We had one that just scraped over the chimneys of our house, I woke up, and mother was kneeling by the bed praying. It kept going, but fell about a mile away and killed twenty-eight people.

I was, fortunately, brought up in a Christian family and had the benefits and blessings. My confirmation service was actually significant for me, I am happy to say, and I still remember my confirmation text from Joshua — 'Have I not commanded thee? Be strong and of a good courage; be not afraid, neither be thou dismayed: for the Lord thy God is with thee whithersoever thou goest.' I've tried to hang on to that in some of the subsequent situations I've found myself in.

It began. One romantic, heady, summer evening . . .

When the war finished I went to school in Highgate and studied art, one modern language, one classical language and one science, which was a nice spread. I horrified the school by telling them I was going to do nursing because they very much wanted me to go to Cambridge to read English. It caused them a certain amount of consternation when the head girl wanted just to be a nurse! There is the privilege of being with people in their most vulnerable moments, you're with them around the clock, and that element of companionship is special to nursing.

I qualified in a London hospital and became engaged in the first seven months or so of clinical nursing. It was the old classic romance story — junior nurse on first night duty, working at a London hospital annex out in the countryside. A patient came in and I had to call the heart surgeon on duty — and that was how it began. One romantic, heady, summer evening in Brentwood, Essex!

Murray and I used to meet for my lunch breaks at midnight in the rhubarb patch. Nobody believed us, but we used to quote poetry to each other. It was a long engagement because in those days it was not the done thing to marry and remain a student nurse. I finished my training on a Thursday afternoon and got married on the Saturday at St Giles in the Fields. We were bell-ringers and my bell-ringing friends came and rang a lovely quarter peel.

We then settled down, with Murray working in General Practice. Robin, our first son was born and I went back to part-time nursing the following year. I then had what I would consider to be the best nursing education any one could have, which was six months as a patient with tuberculosis in Edgware General Hospital. I shall never forget how tough it was. I can remember looking around and just seeing these four walls and thinking, 'I'm not going to see anything else for the next six months.' And worrying about Robin who was only ten months old, back at home. I think the overall learning experience is that I'd have been a much better nurse if I'd known what it was like to be on the receiving end. I became aware of the vulnerability.

**She blurted
out that she
wanted to come
and see me**

What also stands out is how hard it is to assert one's rights and to ask for information when in a dependent role. As compared with an authoritative role, it is important to have advocacy.

Once out of hospital, I needed a career change although I never regretted nursing — it was a wonderful foundation for life. I was busy being a mum with a young family so I read for a BSc in Sociology as a part-time evening student at London University. Essays mingled with carry cots on the dining room table. It was good, because it was a way to use the time of being a full-time mum at home and it gave me something to think about when I was peeling potatoes and washing nappies. It was quite an effort going out for three hours of lectures in the evening, but overall it gave me an appreciation of the privilege of studying. I obtained a First Class Honours, which was useful because it has proved to be an academic 'open Sesame'.

I started my first full-time post as lecturer at the Polytechnic of North London, having no idea what was in store. I got on fine with the students but began to realise that the definition of higher education for the majority of staff in my department was very different from mine. Mine was to encourage students to have the freedom to pursue the truth, but within the parameters of academic rigour and critical evaluation according to the canons of scholarship. Sixteen out of twenty of the academic staff were either hard-line Communist Party or further Left — Marx and Lenin were still fellow-travellers! Students who didn't give the politically correct answer ran a real risk of failure, intimidation and derision.

As things heated up in the heady days of the seventies, I learnt a lot. At that time I was voting Labour, I was not right-wing at all — I had quite an adverse reaction to my Conservative upbringing, especially after nursing in hospitals in the East End of London — I turned into a left-of-centre benign Socialist. However, I soon began to see that things were going on which I could not condone. In the very early days I went into the Ladies cloakroom and a student came in, obviously very distraught and with a look that I was later to see many times in Poland. Checking over her shoulder to make sure there was nobody else within earshot, she blurted out that she wanted to come and see me because she was having difficulty reconciling her study of Sociology with keeping her Christian faith. And I said, 'Of course, you can come and see me any time,' to which she replied, 'I dare not be seen entering your office.' 'Why on earth not?' I asked. And she told me the other staff would take it out on her and ask why she had been to see that Fascist pig? At that stage that was not my self-image, being a Labour voter!

Then we had a lot of occupations. On one occasion, the hardliners in the Polytechnic — mainly staff, but some students — formed an occupation collective, took over one particular part of the Polytechnic in a very comprehensive way and decreed what could be taught each day. I refused to abide by the rules of the occupation collective. It was quite frightening — they really took over the buildings, set bands of vigilantes that went round and broke up teaching not authorised by them.

One morning I had a group of students who had made many sacrifices to come on these courses. In the foyer they had the *agreed* teaching for the day, things like Marxism and the Third World, Marxism and Sex, and the Greenham Common women, absolutely nothing to do with the students' services. I met my group of students and asked them, 'Do you want a class?' They replied, 'Yes, we're desperate, we've got university exams in a few months.' So I told them I was happy to teach them but they had to realise they may well be broken up because it was not authorised, and they said, 'We don't mind — please may we have a class!' So we sat down in the seminar room with no furniture and just myself and a chair to barricade the door. About half an hour later a band of vigilantes came and banged on the door asking, 'What's going on in here?' I replied, 'There's a BSc session of a Criminology seminar.

It's not alternative education so I'm committed to teaching. I intend to continue this seminar and if you want to stop me, you'll have to knock me off my chair. If I get hurt in the process I shall sue the person responsible!' They banged the door shut in their gesture of defiance and shouted, 'We'll be back, dearie.' It took them half an hour to find the courage to come back, but when they did, they knocked me off my chair. They subjected the students to half and hour of the most virulent, vitriolic, verbal abuse — really vicious stuff, just because they wanted a seminar for a course for which they had paid and to which they were entitled.

That, then, was the name of the game of intimidation, character assassination and blackmail. I fought it for nine years and became increasingly disturbed by the wide implications of what was going on, primarily what it did to students. I could literally see how the faces of some students changed. They developed a visible physiognomy of hatred. They became closed-minded and filled with the kind of hair trigger responses of the ideologue. A travesty and antithesis of what higher education should be. On the wider scene, people were being ideologically converted and then fed out into society, into teacher training, into schools, into social work and into the media. This was being used like an ideological forcing house to undermine the principles of democracy. I knew it wasn't just happening at the Poly of North London — it was happening in other places as well.

Eventually, with two colleagues from different departments I wrote a book called *The Rape of Reason — the Corruption of the Polytechnic of North London*, published in 1975. We thought that would be a suicidal act and went back to face the music. But on the day it was due to be published, as I was getting the kids ready for school Murray called up the stairs and said, 'Bernard Levin's on the phone.' I thought he was joking and went on brushing my daughter Pip's hair. Two minutes later Murray called upstairs, 'Are you going to answer the phone, Bernard Levin's hanging on there?!' I suddenly realised it was true and rushed to the phone. He said, 'I have just read your book and I think it's the most important book I've read for ten years. I'm going to deal with it in tomorrow's *Times*.' At that time he did three articles a week in *The Times*. The first one was a very succinct analysis of the book and its implications, entitled in all its brutality, 'The Making of an Intellectual Concentration Camp'. He said, 'Because I think this is such an important book, I am going to devote my remaining two articles this week to discussing it.' That raised people's awareness of the book and probably got me into Margaret Thatcher's sphere of attention, subsequently catapulting me into the House of Lords!

The call to 10 Downing Street came completely out of the blue because I wasn't involved in party politics. I had just written a textbook on Sociology for Nurses, trying to prevent Marxists cornering that neck of the woods, and had handed it in to Butterworths on that Monday morning. I went home to my family in the evening and said, 'I'm sorry I've been a bit occupied with the book. I'm going to cut out all the extras and just enjoy the simple life.' It was lovely while it lasted, for twenty-two hours!

The next day I felt so relaxed. I was then Director of a Nursing Research unit at London University and after work I looked in the phone message book to see if anyone wanted me to play squash, because I still played competitively, and there were the fateful words: 'Please ring 10 Downing Street'. I had no idea what it was about. The next day I phoned the number and a voice said, 'Thank you very much, the Prime Minister would be grateful if you could spare the time to call in and see us in the next day or two.' I dropped the telephone, picked it up again, got my chin off my sternum, and fixed a time for 4.45 pm the next day! I still had no idea what was going on and asked 'Could you please tell me what it's about because while I don't mind coming in with an open mind, I don't like coming with an empty mind!'

I knew it wasn't just happening at the Poly . . .

With shaking knees I steered my way through the door . . .

But they replied, 'No, I'm sorry, we can't.' I arrived at Downing Street, feeling petrified, and waited in the waiting room with my mind a complete whiteout. The doors opened and a charming gentleman greeted me, 'The Prime Minister will see you now.' So with shaking knees I steered my way through the door and into the Presence! She acknowledged me, 'Thank you for coming. Do sit down and I'll come straight to the point. I've read what you have written on education. I've been very impressed by it. I'm just drawing up a list of names to present to Her Majesty with recommendations for life peerages. May I have your permission to put your name on that list?' It was a good thing I was sitting down otherwise I would have done a somersault! She asked me to 'Keep it in confidence because until the Queen has agreed, obviously you can't presume, so please don't tell anybody except your husband, because spouses are different!'

I went home and the kitchen was full of the kids, their friends and neighbours, all saying, 'What happened?' I joked, 'It's much bigger inside Downing Street than it looks outside.' My daughter Pip then asked, 'What did SHE want, Mum?' I said, 'Just a little chat about Education.' As soon as I could, I got my husband down in his consulting room and said, 'It wasn't actually just a chat about Education . . . she offered me a life peerage!' He was absolutely as flabbergasted as I was! I didn't really know what it meant and asked him, 'Do you think it means I'm going to be a Baroness?' He replied, 'When you were a student nurse and I asked you to marry me, I never thought you'd ask me that question!' Then I remembered that in one of the children's bedrooms was a *Children's Encyclopaedia Britannica*. I tiptoed up and found P for Peers of the Realm, tucked it under my arm, went back to Murray's consulting room and from the *Children's Britannica* I learned I was going to be a Baroness!

I was a nurse and social scientist by intention, and a Baroness by astonishment! I have never recovered from the astonishment! Life changed, and I started attending the House of Lords. I was filled with absolute terror and was really apprehensive — I didn't know anybody there. A lot of people come from the House of Commons or from their already established positions with lots of friends and contacts. I came in as a nonentity. Some of the major things I got involved with during the 1980s were on the Education side. I actually moved an amendment to try to prevent political indoctrination in schools and the amendment succeeded. I got over eighty Tory peers to vote against the government. I wasn't the most favourite person, but Margaret Thatcher always said I could speak and vote according to conscience and I did. In 1988 I worked with a number of other peers from all parties to try to reinstate the teaching of Christianity in Religious Education in our schools. Following quite a bit of research I opened a debate on the way in which many of our children were being denied their spiritual heritage.

In the States there is a complete separation of Church and state, but in Britain, in the 1944 Act, it was *enshrined* that children should be taught religious education and it was always *presumed* that that would, at any rate, be the transmission of our Judeo-Christian spiritual heritage. We therefore introduced amendments to the 1988 Education Bill as it was coming up through Parliament to try to ensure that Judeo-Christianity was taught as the main spiritual tradition of this land. Those of other faith communities would have the right for their religions to be taught with respect to the integrity of *their* faiths in the same way as we were trying to respect the integrity of the *Christian faith* for the majority of young people in this land. We had some very, very fierce debates but some wonderful allies. I was actually advised by one of my Muslim friends that the Imam of one of London's largest mosques had led 2,000 Muslims in prayer that the name of Christ would once again be revered in Britain's schools. I quoted that and I couldn't help looking at the Bishops' Bench and saying 'And I would that our Bishops could be heard praying the same prayer!' There were some Bishops who did come out in strong support and, in due course, the Bishop of London undertook to run with the amendments which eventually came on the Statute Book under his leadership. But there were some very hot and challenging times before we got to that stage.

I've never quite recovered from the shock at being catapulted into the House of Lords. I say it is God's sense of humour because I wasn't in politics and while I don't particularly like politics as such, I certainly don't like *party* politics. But of course the House of Lords is a marvellous place to speak for those who cannot speak for themselves, insofar as in Christian Solidarity Worldwide we try to be a 'voice for the voiceless'. It is a very significant arena in which to be able to put the case for those who are suffering from violations of human rights or, in this country, maybe speak for the vulnerable, who find it hard to be advocates for themselves. In more practical terms, with a strange title like a 'Baroness' you tend to get invited, for example, to be patron of organisations, and one of my earliest invitations was to be patron of the Medical Aid for Poland fund. I said, 'I am honoured and delighted, but I don't just want to be a name on the paper. I would like, as appropriate, to travel on the trucks with the aid, for two reasons, one, to ensure it really *does* reach those people in need in Poland and doesn't get hijacked by communists, but also to be able to come back and say, "I've been, I've seen, this is how it *really* is."' I want, not only to speak, but also to be an activist in ways which perhaps would be less likely without that strange title. One of the things that made me most sad was visiting people trapped in a *huge* prison of the former Soviet Empire, suffering from lack of freedom, and then coming back here and finding so many people taking freedom for granted. A lot of people in our institutions, in Education and elsewhere were trying to *impose* a system, which would lead to that kind of deprivation of freedom. The shock of seeing the *reality* of Marxism and Leninism and then the attempt to impose it in a free world was an extraordinarily disturbing and challenging experience.

Many times we had the most wonderful experiences in Poland and always came back so humbled by their three main characteristics — their humour, their generosity, (they had *nothing* and would give you *everything*) and their courage. I've seen those characteristics again and again with people in extreme conditions. Some of the most moving stories of courage I ever heard were in a children's hospital in Krakow. It's hard to imagine that a country in the Continent of Europe could be so deprived and destitute as Poland was. There was literally *nothing* in the hospitals.

We had an urgent message at University Hospital in Warsaw for bandages, needles, syringes, incontinence pads, medicines, you name it — they didn't exist. I was in an Oncology unit with small children and the doctors and nurses had nothing; sometimes they had a few supplies in from the West but they didn't have paediatric-sized needles. They'd spend hours trying to get adult-sized needles into babies' and children's veins. I remember commenting to some mothers how brave their children were and they said, 'Well, some children are brave,' and told me an apparently true story of a twelve-year-old boy. During the Warsaw uprising, in the middle of all the bombing, with the tanks coming and people dying all around him and his own death probably imminent, he wrote these words on a wall: 'I believe in the sun, even when I cannot see it; I believe in love even when I cannot feel it.' That was so true of the Polish people. I never saw hatred in their faces, and they showed love even when it must have been very hard not to hate.

One incident that particularly stays with me is travelling on a 32-tonne truck with medical aid to Poland It was the 100th truck and I *knew* that there would be a special reception and that the Roman Catholic Bishop would be meeting and welcoming us. As we arrived with our

I believe in the sun, even when I cannot see it

'Thank you' is not a word that would come to my lips

truck I just had a great *embarrassment*, a crisis of confidence. I thought, what an asymmetrical situation. Here are we in the West with such abundance. How awful for the Bishop who is a far more educated and cultured person than I will *ever* be, having to stand there with empty hands just waiting. And I thought I couldn't bear it if he said 'thank you'. So as soon as the truck arrived and he graciously came to meet us and started to express his thanks I said, 'Bishop, please do not say thank you. It is our privilege to be able to come with this truck. It is our privilege and our good fortune to be living in a country, which has a surplus. We can offer to be of some help, but it's not altruism. This is our investment in our long-term future because as we in the West become more materialistic, cynical and more humanistic, we will find our spiritual salvation in the suffering Church. So, *please don't say thank you.* You *are* our spiritual salvation.'

When we are with the persecuted Church we have a great privilege of seeing *grace* and *living faith* in a much more vibrant form. My husband, Murray, gave me a quotation: 'Only where there is great danger can there flourish that which saves.' And we see the Church, *'that which saves'*, in great danger, but flourishing. We see the miracles of *grace*, and maybe they are harder to find when a church is *not* in danger, when people have comfortable lives. We may find situations where these things can flourish in the West, where people have a terminal illness or have been extremely heroic in various kinds of tragic circumstances. But they tend to be *personal* circumstances, whereas the persecuted Church faces a *collective* threat to survival and therefore experiences perhaps, the more *visible* and the more *multiple* miracles of grace.

One example of the miracles of grace happened in Nogorno-Karabakh. A village had been overrun by troops who carried out a terrible massacre. They had sawn off the heads of forty-five villagers — we actually saw the buckets-full of swords lying in a ditch — they'd burned others alive, they'd looted and pillaged and ransacked and burnt the homes. When we arrived there, it *was* a place of Golgotha. I went to the hospital and met the head nurse. In this massacre, she had seen her son's head sawn off in front of her and she'd lost fourteen of her extended family.

I wept with her because there were no words adequate for a time like that, but after she'd finished her convulsive sobbing I thought it might be some comfort, some catharsis, to be able to tell the world what had happened to her family, her people. I asked if she wanted to give a message to the world from those who were cut off, and whom nobody knew, and she said, yes, she would. I got out my notebook and pencil and expected a message of grief and bitterness. I could have understood the rage and hatred, but instead, all she said was (and her facial expression changed completely to one of great dignity), 'I just want to say thank you. I'm a nurse. I've worked in this hospital. I've seen how the medicines you have brought have saved many lives and eased a lot of pain. So all I want to say is thank you to all those people who have not forgotten us in these terrible days.' I know 'thank you' is not a word that would come to my lips within hours of seeing my son's head sawn off, but that is what I call, their *miracles of grace*. They *transcend* any human response.

Sometimes all you can say to people in those extreme conditions are, 'I'll take your grief in my heart.' And you do. And it hurts. That having been said, we come back to our comfort zones. We come back to our families. We come back to all the good quality of life we have, at least in terms of this world, in our own countries. They're still there, living in those dark and terrible conditions. Although they are *confined* to those conditions, they still show a radiance of face. They still smile the famous Sudanese smile, they still joke with the famous Armenian wit, and

I think if they can still smile, and they can still joke and they can still be radiant while they are *living* in those conditions, it's not for me to indulge in the self-indulgence of morbid grief when I get back. So I acknowledge the grief, obviously, but I try not to let it impair the effectiveness of what we try to do or to get me down, to use a colloquial phrase, because I think it's not worthy of them.

I joined CSW in 1990 and was asked to become a member of the Board of Management. I wasn't *looking* for anything extra to do, but I think if God opens a door in front of you, you ought to go through it so you can find what he's got in mind on the other side! So I said to them, 'I'll come to one meeting and see if I've got anything to offer!' At the meeting I was so immediately struck by the integrity, commitment and spirituality of that small group of people that I was committed. Things have changed a bit since the early days and the way in which I now formulate our philosophy. We are a very distinctive kind of ministry. We're inter-church — Russian Orthodox, Roman Catholic, I call myself Anglican Unorthodox, Baptist, Pentecostal, Assemblies of God. We work for victims of repression, regardless of creed or colour; we don't proselytise; we are a religious liberty organisation so we respect the rights of people to their own faith. We work according to what we call the principles of the Four 'A's. We are primarily **Advocacy** for human right. We like to ground our advocacy in the **Authenticity** of first-hand evidence, so we try to go to places, not just write about them second-hand, and we try particularly, like the beer advert, *to reach the parts others don't reach*! If a repressive regime victimises minorities within its own borders, the big organisations like the UN, the Red Cross, Save the Children etc, can only go with the permission of a sovereign government. If that sovereign government is denying access to these big organisations, then they can't go and the victims are totally bereft of aid and advocacy. We feel our Christian mandate is to be with some of those who are amongst the most outcast and most suffering, the most neglected in the world. These are the people we try to reach.

It means we have to spend quite a lot of time crossing borders illegally, but we don't believe they are *God's* laws to cut people off like that from all aid and leave people dying of starvation and disease, naked and totally isolated. It is important to be there because, for example, in the Sudan, in the areas designated by the regime as 'no-go' to the big Aid organisations, the world does not know what is going on. We see things the world is not meant to see. When the Sudanese ambassador comes here, talks to British parliamentarians, and says with a sickly smile, 'Of course, we never bomb civilians,' most parliamentarians can't challenge that. I can speak up with, 'Excuse me, your Excellency, I've spent hours in fox-holes while aircraft have been overhead dropping their cargo.' He'll say, 'Well, it's a war, of course we drop bombs, but not on civilians.' But I can produce a photograph of a six-month-old baby with forty percent burns, by a bomb crater and say, 'Is this so, your Excellency?' We're not very popular with those regimes. I think I have a prison sentence passed on me now in Khartoum and I had a price on my head in Azerbaijan. But we believe our work is important.

We mention **Aid** in our work, although we're not primarily an Aid organisation. The fourth 'A' is **Accountability**, primarily to those for whom we speak, to try to make sure that we tell the truth, speak about their situation and are sensitive to their needs, but also *accountable* to our supporters. These then are the four principles on which we work. And every time we go into the field with a mission, we always have three objectives. One is to *obtain first-hand evidence* of violation of human rights and the suffering that people are enduring, in order to present that as advocates. Secondly, *to assess their need for humanitarian aid* and to try to provide that as best we can with our limited resources. It might also be that, through speaking out and being

**The world does
not know what is
going on . . .**

. . . God seems to provide them on many occasions

advocates, we are being able to mobilise other resources, which are beyond our capacity. For example, in Karabakh, at the height of the war, we managed to prevail upon MERLIN (Medical Emergency Relief International) to come in. They did a *wonderful* immunisation programme for children who were in a worse condition that those in Bosnia. We can act as a catalyst for that type of aid. While we're there we are showing our solidarity with people who have felt completely cut off. Very often, when we arrive people come running up with such joy; their first words are 'Thank God you've come. We thought the world had forgotten us. But the fact that we know we're not forgotten gives us the strength to continue to struggle to survive.' And they often say to us that that *solidarity* is the most precious and valuable thing we can give. I can't judge it — I haven't been in that predicament — but we've heard that so often, in so many places, that it seems to ring true, and what a *privilege!*

We work with victimised children and one of our *main* programmes is in the Russian Federation. We wrote a highly critical human rights report stinging the way in which the former Soviet Union abused, totally exploited and took away all human rights from abandoned children. They didn't have proper education; they were used as slave labour or for the army. If they were too independently minded and ran away from the special orphanages, they were sent to psychiatric hospitals and given horrendous drug regimes that used to be given to psychiatric dissidents. I remember one little thin, pointed-faced child, Igor, looking at me with tears in his eyes and saying, '*Please* will you find me a mother? I want to get out of here.' We took back a multi-disciplinary group, educationalists, psychologists, paediatricians, I as a nurse and social scientist, and we did some systematic research. I wrote the report to Directors of Despair and went back to Russia to publish the Russian Language edition expecting a lot of criticism.

Instead, *wonderfully* this was where the miracles began. The directors of the orphanage where we had done our work said, 'Thank you for your research. It's documented what we thought, but couldn't prove.' On the same visit, the Russian Minister of Education invited us to the Kremlin. He said, 'It's documented what we knew but we couldn't articulate within the system. Will you help us set up the first Foster Family Care Programme for the whole of Russia, here in Moscow?' And the miracles began there. We have a motto in CSW — we don't believe in miracles, we *rely* on them! And God seems to provide them on many occasions.

When I pray I try to begin this way, 'Holy Spirit, will you please pray through me,' because I think God must get very tired of us talking *at* him, and then I'm afraid I start to talk at him! I divide my prayers into five; I try to start with *Praise*. I try to say a very heartfelt *Thank You* for the amazing gifts with which he blesses my life. I try to turn to him in *Repentance* and ask for forgiveness and healing. I lift up to him those I love and ask his protection for them. Amongst my husband's last words, on the answer machine the night before he died, were an amazing act of faith, which I admire and cherish. He said, 'All will be well' — that's before he had his cardiac surgery from which he died under anaesthetic. He said, 'All will be well, and whatever happens, all will still be well. All manner of things will be well, and whatever happens, all manner of things will be well.' Then I pray that for all our family and friends whom I love, so *Intercession* for loved ones. And then *Intercession* for those who are suffering, those whom one knows in this country on a personal basis who suffer from illness or old age, trouble, or bereavement. And then a broader prayer, trying to remember the requests to pray for people suffering in the broader arena, including the persecuted Church. I don't leave much time for God after all that! But I do try to be still, and know that he is God. I heard a lovely comment from Mother Teresa on the radio. When she was asked about her prayers, she said, 'I just listen' and when the interviewer asked her, 'Well, what does God say?' she replied,

'Nothing, He just listens too!' I find that very moving and I try to do that. I try to be still. I try to follow that. Not terribly successfully!

They always say that Christianity goes deep in the soul of the Armenian people. In the early days of that brutal ethnic cleansing of Azerbaijan of the Armenians they had something called 'Operation Ring' which was a systematic deportation in which they would surround villages with tanks and helicopters and round everybody up. One of the farmers knew how to escape from the cordon when his village was surrounded by troops, because he knew the hills. I met him two years later and he told me of that terrible day. He said he was feeling awful because of what he'd seen happen to his family and his community. It was May 1991 and the trees were in blossom. He went to one of them for comfort — it was so beautiful. It was an apricot tree and as he got near he saw, to his horror, the body of a five-year-old Armenian girl, cut in two, hanging from a branch; he wept and vowed revenge. As he was telling us this, he wept again and said, 'I feel very bad that I never kept my vow, because later, when we took Azeris villages, I could never bring myself to harm a child, so I broke my promise.' I had an American colleague with me who stood up, took off his baseball cap and said, 'Thank you, sir. For the first time in my life I realise what it means when it says in the Bible, "Vengeance is mine; … saith the Lord", and thank you for the dignity you've shown,' to which this simple farmer, cut off from all the ordinary structures of religion for most of his life, said something unforgettable, 'Dignity is a Crown of Thorns.' So we say our brothers and sisters in Christ are wearing their crown of thorns with great dignity, and they ask for our prayers. Please may we not forget them.

**As he got near
he saw,
to his horror,
the body . . .**

JOHN STOTT
TELLING PEOPLE THE GOOD NEWS

As a secular scientist, my father was very interested in all branches of natural history and was a good amateur botanist. He used to take me for walks in the country during our summer holidays when I was only about five or six and tell me to shut my mouth and open my eyes and ears, which was a great introduction to observation of nature. I started as a butterfly collector and for a small boy, I had a very good collection of butterflies.

One day, in the nursery, one of my sisters threw a cushion at me. It landed in the middle of my precious butterfly collection. If I've ever seen red in my life, I saw it then. I chased her round and round the table in the nursery — I reckon I would have killed her if I'd caught her. But fortunately, she was nimbler than I. I was utterly inconsolable of course, but it's an interesting example of God's providence. Although I couldn't be consoled at the time, and the whole bottom had dropped out of my world, I'm now glad, because I turned to birds. People think me peculiar enough going round the world with binoculars as a bird watcher, but imagine going round the world with a butterfly net!

I very much enjoy bird watching, partly intrinsically, partly because it takes you out into the wilderness. There's almost nothing I love more than getting up with the sun and going out into the paddy fields, into the Australian bush, or into the rain forest with all the sights, the smells and the sounds of nature.

I was born in London in 1921. My father was a physician, and later became senior physician at the Westminster Hospital and Physician to the Royal Household. When I was two years old, we moved to 58 Harley Street, London. As my sisters and I grew up and needed rooms of our own, we moved across Harley Street to No. 65. When my father reached the peak of his medical career he had a chauffeur and a secretary, and we had a cook, a housemaid and a parlour maid.

My mother's mother was German and she was brought up in Lutheran piety. So she taught my sisters and me to say our prayers, read the Bible every day and go to church. My father was not a believer, though he came to church two or three times a year out of solidarity with the family. So I lived in London and funnily enough, I attended All Souls Church as a small boy. Sitting in the gallery, and being somewhat mischievous in those days, I used to make pellets out of bus tickets and drop them on to the fashionable hats of the ladies below. Little did I imagine that I would one day occupy the pulpit of that same church!

I was sent to a boarding school at the tender age of eight and later to Rugby School and it was there, at the age of nearly seventeen, that I first understood the gospel in a personal way, and received Christ as my Lord and Saviour. I was invited to attend what, today, would be called a Christian Union meeting, run by boys for boys in the school, with no masters around at all. I started attending regularly on Sunday afternoons. I had been going a number of months when we heard a visiting speaker who was an Anglican clergyman, the Rev E. J. H. Nash. He preached that afternoon, if my memory is right, on Pilate's question, 'What shall I do, then, with Jesus who is called Christ?' It hit me between the eyes, because I never knew I had to *do* anything with Jesus who is called Christ. He was part of the furniture of my mind, but the idea that I had to do anything about it was quite new. So I asked Mr Nash some

If I've ever seen red in my life . . .

questions afterwards and he had the spiritual discernment to see that I was a seeker. He took me out for a drive in his car and answered my questions.

He read Revelation 3:20, in which Jesus says, 'Behold, I stand at the door, and knock. If anyone hears my voice and opens the door, I will come in . . .' Mr Nash was wise enough not to precipitate a decision. I had the whole of that afternoon and evening to think about it and to count the cost.

That night, at about 9.30 when the other boys were in bed in the dormitory, I crept out of bed, knelt at my bedside, and told Jesus I had made a mess of my life so far. I thanked him for his death on the cross insofar as I understood it, opened the door, and asked him to come in. I saw no flash of lightning, I heard no peals of thunder, no electric shock passed through my body, and so I hopped into bed and went to sleep. But the following morning, I knew that something had happened — I didn't know what — it took me some weeks, even months, really to understand the difference between being religious and being a Christian, but something had happened.

I put it in my diary at the time that Christ, who had been *outside* the door, was now inside. I'd said my prayers to him through the keyhole; I'd pushed pennies under the door to keep him quiet, but now I'd opened the door and he'd come in and that was the essential difference. I can *still* remember walking down the street at Rugby one day, and this is not an exaggeration — I can only say that suddenly an awareness was given to me that I had no enemies any longer and that I was in love with the world! Mr Nash nurtured me and was incredibly faithful. He wrote to me once a week for five years and I know he prayed for me every day. That was in 1938, the year before war broke out.

My father went straight into the Army Medical Service as a Major General, while I, who was only a year old as a Christian, could only describe myself as an instinctive pacifist. I had read the Sermon on the Mount for the first time through Christian eyes and it didn't seem to me *conceivable* that Christians should engage in killing and in retaliating. So, you can understand that a serious rift developed in my family in that my father simply couldn't accept having a pacifist son. I didn't have to go before a conscientious objector tribunal because I had indicated to the Headmaster of Rugby, more than six months before war broke out, that I believed God had called me into the ordained ministry. I was granted an exempt status and was actually up at Cambridge as a student through most of the war.

When I got up to Cambridge, the first part of my tripos, as we called the degree, was in Modern Languages. During the holidays while I was at Rugby, I had spent a month every summer either in France or in Germany. It was generally understood in the family that, because of these languages, I would go into the Diplomatic or Foreign Service.

After I had come to Christ, however, the idea of spending my life in the realm of diplomatic compromise no longer appealed to me. I was astonished that I had reached the age of seventeen without, so far as I know, having heard the gospel. And so it was natural, because of my own experience, that I wanted to spend the rest of my life telling people the good news that I had not heard until I was seventeen.

The war ended and six months later, in December 1945, I was ordained in St Paul's Cathedral by the Bishop of London. I served my curacy, my first pastorate, as an assistant at All Souls, Langham Place. It actually happened in the most casual way. I was at Ridley Hall doing Theology and had recently graduated. During a special service I was asked to read John 3:1–16 by Rev Harold Earnshaw-Smith. After the service, he came straight up to me and said, 'Are you fixed for a curacy? Why don't you come to All Souls?' So I said, 'Fine, it sounds great to me!'

> **I'd pushed pennies under the door to keep him quiet**

Within about six months of my ordination, Earnshaw-Smith had his first coronary thrombosis. So I was very much thrown in at the deep end. He came back after a few months, but he later had a second and then a third coronary which killed him in 1950. I was left partly in charge of the parish and to my, and everybody's astonishment, was appointed to succeed him. So, at the tender age of 29 I became Rector of All Souls, Langham Place and had the great privilege of seeking to put into practice some of the principles of evangelism, lay training and lay ministry, which I had learned and cherished at Cambridge. By the year 2000, I had been attached to All Souls Church for fifty-five years — five years as curate, twenty-five years as Rector, and the rest of the time as Rector Emeritus.

One of the first things I did as Rector was to determine that on one Sunday evening a month, we would have what I called a 'Guest Service'. The congregation would be encouraged to bring non-Christian guests. They *knew* there would be a straightforward exposition of the gospel and a description of the steps to Christ *with an opportunity* to respond. That meant we would need counsellors. So, if we were to have counsellors who would speak to the people who came forward, they would need some training, which led to the start of a training school. It lasted for twelve weeks each year, six lectures on the gospel and six on the practice of evangelism. At the end of the course, we set a written examination and those who passed were commissioned by the Bishop and became what we called 'Commissioned Workers'.

Biblical or expository preaching, would be another priority for us. I had, from my childhood onwards, a conviction about the uniqueness and inspiration of the Bible so I saw the great need to use the pulpit for its exposition and application. Although I started with a vision of biblical exposition, I came to see that it wasn't enough to *expound* the Bible and leave the text up in the air, but that application was as necessary as exposition. I used to say rather piously that I expound the text and I leave to the Holy Spirit the work of application. But I came to see that we are responsible for both.

I had a very formative experience in the early seventies when I was talking to two students. They had both been brought up in a Christian home, now one was at Oxford and the other at Edinburgh, and both were repudiating the faith of their parents. When I asked them why was it that they no longer believed that Christianity was true, they said, 'No, that's not our problem, and if you could *persuade* us that Christianity is true, we're not at all sure that we would accept it.' 'Oh', I said with surprise, 'so what is your problem?' 'Our problem,' they said, 'is not whether Christianity is true but whether Christianity is *relevant*, and frankly we don't see how it can be.' These were their exact words: 'Christianity is a primitive Palestinian religion. It arose in a primitive Palestinian culture, so what on earth has it got to say to us who live in the exciting modern world?' Then they became excited and enthused with the modern world. They said, 'We have men on the moon in the seventies; we shall have men on Mars in the eighties. [They were a bit optimistic!] We have transplant surgery today and will have genetic engineering tomorrow.' And then, with a sneer, almost a leer, they said, 'What has your primitive Palestinian religion got to say to us? It's irrelevant!'

I've often thanked God for that experience, because it challenged me, as I'd never been challenged before, to the task of bridging the gulf between the biblical world and the modern world. In 1982 I wrote a book called *I Believe in Preaching*. In the US its title is *Between Two Worlds*. For preaching is essentially bridge building, relating the Word to the world — the ancient Word to the modern world. This led to *The Bible Speaks Today* series, whose purpose is to expound Scripture, to relate it to modern issues and to be readable.

What on earth has it got to say to us?

I'm distressed by the disunity . . .

This in turn led to the founding of the London Institute for Contemporary Christianity, which has the same purpose — building bridges between the Word and the world. 'Contemporary Christianity', which is rather a mouthful, is not some new brand of Christianity that we're busy inventing. It is in fact orthodox, historic, biblical Christianity sensitively related to the modern world.

I started writing when I was Head Boy of Rugby School, editing one of the School magazines and having to write a brief editorial in each issue. But the first book I wrote was at the invitation of the Bishop of London. When he instituted me to All Souls as Rector in 1950, he urged me to go on studying and writing, and urged the churchwardens to give me time in which to do so. Four years later, he followed this up by inviting me to write what was then called, 'The Bishop of London's Lent Book'. He commissioned somebody every Lent to write a book that the church people were encouraged to read as part of their Lenten discipline. I wrote the book *Men with a Message*, which was an attempted introduction to the New Testament authors and their writings. Almost everything I have written has first been either preached or lectured.

In 1971, I set up the Evangelical Literature Trust, mainly in order to recycle my royalties. It seemed to me appropriate that money raised through the writing of books should be recycled in the distribution of books in the developing countries of the Third World. Travel in the Third World had introduced me to the appalling poverty of millions. It seemed obvious that we who live in affluence *must* simplify our economic lifestyle, not because this will solve the macro-economic problems of the world, but out of solidarity with the poor. Now my contribution is accompanied by gifts from trusts.

As I look into the new Millennium and the future of the church, I'm distressed by the disunity of the evangelical constituency. It has often been said that we're no longer a party, but a coalition. God has caused the evangelical movement to grow enormously in the last fifty years. We've grown in numbers, in theology, and in influence. But we *do not* have the influence we *ought* to have in the church or in the nation because of our disastrous divisions.

I wish we could learn that the things that unite us as evangelical people are much more than the things that divide us, and that we should be able to agree to work together, without compromising any fundamental truth, of course. I believe that the quest for the visible unity of the church is a proper Christian goal, but not unity at the expense of truth. John's Gospel, Chapter 17, has often been misused in the ecumenical movement, as if Jesus prayed only for unity, '. . . Father that they may be one, as we are one', etc. But actually Jesus prayed for four things. He prayed *first* for the truth of the church, that God would keep his followers *true* to his name; secondly he prayed for the *holiness* of the church, that they may be delivered from evil and thirdly he prayed for the *mission* of the church, 'as you sent me . . . I have sent them into the world', and fourthly he prayed for *unity*.

So if we are to be balanced, we need to be concerned simultaneously with the truth, holiness, mission and unity of the church. There have been many movements in the church that have gone for one or other of those four, without keeping them together.

The greatest challenge to the church in the new Millennium, I think, is 'pluralism'. Pluralism is not just asserting the fact that there is a plurality of faiths in the world. Pluralism is itself an ideology that affirms the validity of *every* religion; that every religion is true. So if we insist on proclaiming the uniqueness and finality of Jesus Christ, we will undoubtedly suffer for it.

MICHAEL JONES

When I was just four years old my dad passed away suddenly from a heart attack. He was only thirty-eight years of age. I can still remember the day very clearly. A policeman was at our home, which was a bit of thrill, but I suppose he was only there because he was going through the procedures of a sudden death. That night my mother got our family together, and as we knelt at the side of the bed she thanked the Lord that our dad had gone to be with him.

At the funeral she told the congregation not to be sorrowful but just to celebrate his life. It was a very Christian funeral and it had a big impact on me. I was immersed in a family full of love, and my mother, who was very much a God-fearing woman, instilled Christian values in me from the time I was born. I am very thankful for that wonderful upbringing.

It wasn't until I was seven that I actually asked the Lord into my life as my own personal Saviour, at a Good News Club. I knew God was real — there was no doubt about it even as a young child. I could see God's love through the people around me, through the experiences I had, especially when my father passed away, and I just knew he was real. It was a simple child-like act of faith, but although I was very young it has kept me on the straight and narrow for most of my life.

I was overawed to be asked by this renowned, super coach

Rugby was something that came naturally to me, and as a seven-year-old I dreamt of being an All Black. I had my childhood heroes, one in particular, a Samoan called Brian Williams — he was the Jonah Lomu of rugby back in the seventies. Being part-Samoan (my father was Kiwi and my mother, Samoan) I could say, 'If Brian Williams can do it, why can't I?' so I had many dreams of playing for the All Blacks.

My mum always encouraged and supported that side of my life. I played my first game of rugby for the local club when I was five years old. I was barefoot and it was in the middle of winter but that's how we do it in New Zealand. My support crew — my mum, my sisters, and my uncles and aunties — came on Saturdays to cheer me on.

Sunday was a day that we as a family always put aside as the Lord's Day. We went to church and then spent the day together resting and focusing more on the things of God. When I moved into my teenage years there was pressure from coaches and managers to play rugby on Sunday. They knocked on our door and asked my mum if they could take me to some trials or something for the local rep teams. My mum very politely declined their requests and because I just couldn't imagine playing sport on a Sunday, I wasn't fazed by it. As I got older there was a lot more pressure, especially as I began to excel, and big-time coaches wanted me to represent my province at senior level.

After one of my games the All Black coach at the time asked me exactly where I stood on the Sunday issue. He told me that I had the potential, but not being able to play on Sunday could be a real issue that could preclude me from further opportunities. Even though I was overawed to be asked by this renowned, super coach, I did not have any trouble sticking to my convictions. I told him where I stood and said that if it was going to be an obstacle to further selection then I was quite prepared for that.

Looking back, it is amazing the way God has honoured that decision because from that day, the door has always stayed open. I was first selected to play for Auckland in 1985 and then the All Blacks in 1987. That year I played in my first World Cup in New Zealand.

MICHAEL JONES

It will always be special because it was my first year as an All Black and I was playing in an awesome team of individuals who were all at their peak. We set new standards in rugby and of course the greatest thrill was to win the cup!

I'm very proud and privileged to play for my country; it means a lot to me. I've often been asked, 'If it means so much to you, how do you justify, as a Christian, not playing for your country on a Sunday.' I tell them, 'Compared to the Lord dying on the cross for my sins and giving me eternal life, my sacrifice is nothing.' As I was growing up I had to make that decision for myself. My mum left it up to me and it was very much a conviction that I wanted to continue to honour the Lord by honouring his day. Every Christian has a story to tell and I believe it is something that the Lord requires *of me*. I have friends who do play on Sunday and go to the same church and share the same faith, but this is *my* story — this is the way I believe the Lord would have *me* lead *my* life.

There was a time when, through different circumstances, I started to compromise a bit. I wasn't really rebellious, but it took a serious knee injury to get me back on track. I'd been an All Black for two years and things were going well. We were playing Argentina when it happened. Instead of picking up the ball and running for it, I thought I might kick it forward and then pick it up. I saw a big opening for a try, but it didn't work out that way! As I went to kick the ball, a guy caught me and hit my leg at just the wrong angle. I ruptured all the ligaments in my knee. It was a very serious injury and could be compared to being hit by a car doing 50 km an hour. At the snap of a finger my whole career was brought to a halt.

We were playing Argentina when it happened

I woke up the next morning after the operation and read in the newspapers: 'Thanks, Michael Jones, for the memories.' People said, 'Poor Michael, we'll never see him again. It's over.' But it was an amazing time in my life. My mum asked if she could pray over the hands of the surgeon for God's help and he was kind enough to let her do that. It was a very successful operation, but healing was a slow process and the prognosis was that it was very unlikely I would ever play rugby again. Suddenly, I was on my back and my entire world had crumbled in terms of sport and my career. It was time for reflection and I was forced to re-examine where I was in my relationship with the Lord. I found spiritual and physical healing and within thirteen months I was back playing rugby for Auckland. A couple of months later I was reselected to play for the All Blacks on their tour of France in 1990.

I continued to have many more injuries and was eventually nicknamed 'Ice' or 'Iceman'. I'm not sure if this came from the fact that, after each game, I have to apply ice to every part of my body (almost!), or because I have a reputation for not losing my cool on the field! My attitude, going into any game, is to go hard out and give it my best. However, I like to play from the rules. Tackling is a very important part of rugby now and it is a big part of any team's game plan to have an offensive defence. I've always taken a lot of pride in ensuring that, when I tackle, I tackle hard and in a clean way. That's going to benefit our team because sometimes it's the only way to turn a ball and nullify a team's attacking moves. I am often asked how a Christian can hand out such fearsome tackling and an easy reply is, 'It is better to give than to receive!' Obviously it's not in that context and people see the humorous side of it! More importantly, I want to use my gifts to glorify the Lord, because whenever we go out that's my number one goal. It has always been my desire in playing rugby that through just being there people might get a glimpse of the glory of God. Not so much in anything fantastic that I am able to do, but maybe just in my approach to the game.

I have had a long, successful career and rugby has been my life . . . but not all of it. The desire of my heart has always been to put God first and I've found that everything else falls into place — my relationship with my wife Maliena, my family, the people around me and the things that I'm involved in. As Christians we're not promised a life that is a bed of roses. We have trials and tribulations. We go through the valleys and this helps us to enjoy the mountaintop but I've found that through everything God has been faithful in so many ways. He's never left me nor forsaken me. I've had my fair share of personal loss. My parents have both passed away, my mum, tragically, a few years ago in a car accident when she was in Kenya for my step-brother's wedding. She was a very great influence in my life and we were a very close family, so that was a huge loss. Maliena had three miscarriages before we had a baby. But God's been faithful. He's always come through for me and it's through those times that we've grown closer.

When I held my little girl for the first time, the rugby and the greatest experience of winning a test match for my country was actually pale in comparison! The Lord's been gracious and words can't explain how much I love him.

I've had my fair share of personal loss

Japanese people were disillusioned with what happened after World War II. Many of the things they had been taught when they were young were declared to be wrong so they had to adapt to a new philosophy and world-view. Emperor worship was proved wrong and suddenly the whole populace began to embrace materialism. I was born in 1947 and as I grew up my father taught me atheism. He taught me to trust myself and only the things I could see and touch. As a result I despised people who had any kind of religion, including Christianity.

I was shocked when I discovered he was a Christian

My home was very poor so my dream in life was to attain material success. In order to reach that goal I knew I needed a good college education and to become an employee of a prestigious company. I had a particular interest in the English language so I went to High school in California as a foreign exchange student for one year. My host family were Mormon and although I was an atheist, to harmonise with their lifestyle I attended their church for the year but never embraced their faith. However, I felt I needed to investigate what the Bible had to say when I had more time.

I returned to Japan, studied hard and gained entrance to a well-known university in Tokyo. I should have been happy, but the more I thought about the meaning of my life, the more disappointed I became. I had a strong conviction that everything would end at my death and as I pondered this I lost hope and direction. After a difficult first year I entered my sophomore year with a new roommate. He was a year younger than I, but he was a completely different person. In those days we stayed up very late, and got up late in the morning — so I probably missed the first class. I only cleaned my room about once or twice a year — it was a very messy lifestyle. However, this guy got up very early, cleaned his room and sat at his desk to read his Bible and pray. I was shocked when I discovered he was a Christian. I decided to visit his church, not because I was particularly interested in the Bible, but because I was interested in his personality. I wanted to find out what made him the person he was. Over the next two years as I attended the church I struggled emotionally as well as intellectually with the biblical worldview of an almighty God. Finally, at a Campus Crusade for Christ camp, I discovered the true meaning of Jesus and the cross. The preacher said that Jesus died for us, for our sin, because he loved us so much. I burst into tears, crying uncontrollably, and when I stopped I knew I was reconciled to my Heavenly Father through the love of Jesus Christ.

After graduation I sensed a call from the Lord to full-time ministry. I didn't have sufficient faith or commitment to follow that urging so instead I became a businessman and worked for a major textile company. Two years later, McDonald's came to Japan. I knew that the hamburger business would be a success in this country, so I decided to join them. I worked for four years as a purchasing manager and as the business flourished I became very successful. My income was increasing every year and I seemed to have everything that I wanted, but a strange thing happened. The higher the position I attained and the more money I accumulated, the less love I embraced toward Jesus Christ, who previously had been so dear to me. At one point the Holy Spirit spoke to my heart and asked me the tough question: 'Do you serve money or do you serve the Lord, the one true God?'

KENICHI NAKAGAWA

The scandal was a painful experience . . .

At that point, I remembered God's call to Christian ministry. I tremblingly confessed to my wife Fumia that I felt this was what God was asking me to do, and asked her to join me. She replied, 'I have been praying for that decision ever since we got married!' That was the confirmation I needed. I left McDonald's and commenced a three-year course at Trinity Evangelical Divinity School in Illinois. During that time, being Japanese, I probably spent more time than the American students just reading books — it took time. While I was studying, Fumia watched some Christian TV and was very surprised by the variety of Christian ministries. When we began to watch together I was impressed, because I knew the power of the mass media, the power of TV. When McDonald's in Japan started airing commercial spots, sales doubled immediately! One day while watching a preacher I suddenly saw my face on the TV screen, preaching to my own people! I had no money, no connections, no experience, no knowledge about the TV industry in Japan but somewhere in my heart I knew that the Holy Spirit had spoken to me and told me this was what I was going to do for my people when I went back to Japan!

The week I returned, Jim Bakker's PTL Club office was established in Japan and I was invited to join their TV ministry! During the first year I was an assistant preacher and then became the main preacher on the programme for five or six years. This was an indigenous programme with foreign financial support. Two years prior to the Jim Bakker scandal being revealed, I sensed that I should leave and start another TV ministry with the financial help of local Japanese churches and Christians. The scandal was a painful experience, but for me the PTL Club did a lot of good things. They gave me experience in TV ministry and, in a sense, our Harvest Time ministry is a spin-off. There is another programme called Life Line, which is also a continuation, so in spite of negative and tragic incidents God has provided us with two indigenous TV ministries.

When Harvest Time Ministries commenced, I received encouraging words from almost all the local pastors. They remarked that I was treading a difficult path, and if I were still there after three months, it would be a miracle! By the Lord's grace and the support of Japanese Christians, we have been on the air for thirteen years and have about fourteen stations which air our weekly programme. At the beginning of the TV ministry, airtime was difficult and expensive to purchase and the TV stations were only interested in viewing rates and the money they could make. Religious programmes were relegated to marginal spots, but as we enter the age of satellite digital TV it should be easier and we will be airing a one-hour programme every day instead of only thirty minutes once a week. I am hoping that we will be able to launch a whole Christian channel within a few years. We established a local office in California and have stations in Hawaii, Los Angeles and New York that air our programme to the Japanese speaking communities.

In the west, there's a term 'TV Evangelist' or 'Tele-evangelist' which sometimes carries a negative connotation. In Japan we cannot request funds directly on TV and don't therefore have such a term. I do itinerant evangelism and work very closely with churches all over Japan because that's the only way that our ministry has any meaning. Once people become interested and want to read the Bible we refer them to their local churches. Sometimes people call me a TV pastor, but I don't want to use that term because a pastor is someone who is living with his people, and I cannot pastor people through television.

The system in Japan is collapsing. In the past it didn't matter whether something looked good or evil, people had to accept both at the same time for creating harmony, even on the issue of 'truth'. This kind of thinking is going out of the window because they are beginning to see that they have to function according to the truth — according to a higher value system, otherwise our country will have no standing or be competitive among world leaders. So I think the issue of relativism versus one ultimate value system is becoming very clear to the Japanese mind and, especially now, we have a chance of presenting a system acceptable to most of them. I think, *experientially*, the Japanese people are losing confidence in their own thinking and are beginning to search for the answer outside of themselves. That is probably one of the reasons why a book such as *The Book of God: The Bible as a Novel*, published in Japanese, is selling so well. In one year it has sold more than 450,000 copies and has become one of the best sellers, with the business people buying it. It would seem therefore, that the message of the Almighty God is beginning to make sense to many Japanese people.

Statistically speaking, we don't see immediate change yet, but careful observation of what is happening reveals several positive signs. A common phenomenon throughout Japan is that the presence of men within the church is increasing. Japanese Christian leaders are sharing their testimony boldly. When we were economically successful Christians kept quiet, but now they are beginning to share their faith in the midst of difficult situations. I have interviewed several leading Christian business people, one of them a Vice-president of a large cosmetic company in Japan, and another the Chairman of a major Japanese bank, who openly shared their faith on TV, which was quite unknown before.

However, we still need to be very sensitive about how we handle the Japanese culture. If we approach our culture through western eyes, many of our traditions and practices look very bad and seem to be associated with idol worship. Western missionaries often made the mistake of denying the Japanese culture altogether. Although without a doubt there are things that are heavily associated with idol worship, there are other areas that are positive and afford the means to praise the Lord. Japanese people have the right and responsibility to praise the Lord within their own cultural matrix. There are intermediate areas where we need to redeem the culture by giving a biblical meaning to their traditions. Japanese festivities are closely associated with farming, cultivation and harvesting, similar to Old Testament festivities. The difference is that the object of thanksgiving, or worship, is different. Japanese people don't know to whom they should give thanks. But the festivities have thanksgiving at their heart and so, rather than denying the whole thing as idol worship, I think we need to direct that feeling of appreciation towards the right Deity and provide the biblical perspective rather than denying the whole thing.

When I first met Jesus, he was a person who died for me because he loved me so much. As my appreciation for him has deepened, he showed himself to be the High Priest who is interceding for me at the right hand of God. As the years have passed, I have begun to appreciate the meaning of the Trinity, Father, Son and Holy Spirit. How beautiful it is that three persons can exist in such harmony and love. The human mind could never create a God of that nature. It has to be God who reveals himself. As I think about Jesus, I increasingly think about his humility and how he died to show his love for us.

I am helping an old lady who has a son and a daughter. The lady and her daughter became believers but the son is prodigal. He is in his middle forties and likes gambling. He borrows money and many times his mother has had to pay his debts. His wife has left him and he is alone so he is asking for his mother's real estate to be given to him. She comes to Christian meetings with scars, bruises and tears because he has been beating and kicking her for five or six years. When she asks for prayer and counselling I tell her, 'He's an adult. He should be responsible for his life. You are making things worse by continually letting him off the hook.

**Western
missionaries
often made the
mistake . . .**

Tell him that he's on his own from now on, that you're going to live your life, and he should live his life.' She agrees, 'That's right, that's right, yes, yes' — but she never does it! Every time she comes back with the same problem and I wonder why she is so reluctant to break off with her son. Then I began to realise that it is *because she loves him*. Look at this country! God can judge this country immediately because of what we are doing, but he doesn't! Japanese people think that God is weak! Why doesn't he judge them? Because he loves the Japanese. Jesus died for us *because he loves us so much*. If you understand that I think the only meaningful response is, 'Thank you, I love you too.'

I wonder why she is so reluctant to break off with her son

I was born in India — both sides of my family are British and lived out there. It was all part of the British Raj but we left when home rule came in because the British were perhaps not as welcome then as they had been. My father quite wisely said, 'Let's uproot and go.' He wanted to go to Australia, but my mother said if he did he would be on his own, because she was taking the children back home to Blighty!

So in September 1948 we returned to England and if it hadn't been for some family members I don't know what would have happened to us because we had nothing here. My father had a really good job with Kelners in India. They supplied all his needs — the company paid for his home, the food, people who washed up, and maids. When he finally sold all his possessions to come back to England, we arrived with £5.00 sterling. There was nothing else in the coffers.

My grandmother kept us for a year and then my aunt kept us for another couple of years. We lived in abject poverty. A neighbour said, 'This is impossible. There are six of you living in one room?' It was our kitchen, dining room, toilet, bedroom — she got a local councillor to come and see the situation. Having seen us, we were pushed to the top of the waiting list, and within a matter of months we had our first council house of our own. It was bare, devoid of anything at all, so we slept on the floor on mattresses for quite a while.

I like remembering those days because quite often, people like myself are written off because we have money. It is thought that if a person has money, they have no opinions, if fame, well, who cares what you think! It's as though we're dehumanised in some way and I *hate* that feeling. I like to remind people that my memories are totally intact when it comes to the poverty I lived through. So I feel that, by remembering those days, I keep very much in touch with the reality that unfortunately still is with us. There are people who live in poverty and it's a terrible indictment on society that we still have people around who don't seem to be able to help themselves.

I became a Christian in 1966. I'd spent three years discussing, no, arguing belligerently against it all. No one tries to prove Christianity right, they all try to prove it wrong so we can move on to the next philosophy or the next religion and deal similarly with that.

People had told me that Christianity was really a relationship. I could never understand that but someone told me to read Revelation 3:20: 'Behold, I stand at the door and knock.' And to me, that *picture* of someone standing outside the door of my life and banging on it rang bells! It was then a matter of slowly discovering the simple fact that Jesus stands outside of our lives wanting to come into them, and all I had to do was say, 'Come in!'

When I became a Christian I wasn't worried about losing my success and career as a pop star but I was warned about it. I had been asked to give a testimony at a Billy Graham rally in 1966 and certain people said, 'If you're going to make this public statement you have to be aware of one thing. You could be derided out of the country and out of your career. It's not the most popular thing to say that you're a Christian.' I thought to myself, if I really believe this and if it is true, then surely it's more important than anything else — it *has* to be more important than my career. And so I decided, Yes, I *will* go on the platform. I *need* to say it. I *need* to confess him with my lips. I took that opportunity, and thankfully it didn't end my career.

It was our kitchen, dining room, toilet, bedroom . . .

Instead, having made my public declaration of faith, that Christmas I did a pantomime at the London Palladium that broke all the box office records known to the theatre. So I thought, 'Well perhaps God does want me here after all!'

I have used my career *unashamedly*. I haven't cheated the public. I've always told them when I was doing a Gospel tour and when it's 'Cliff speaks and sings about his faith, please do not expect "Congratulations" or "Bachelor Boy"'. But Christianity does influence the choice of songs I record. I don't choose Christian songs all the time but I try *not* to sing songs that would bring any kind of dishonour. If I feel that there are lyrics a Christian shouldn't sing then I try to change them. I did it with a song called 'Devil Woman'. There was nothing wrong with the story line — it was like Edgar Alan Poe really — a story about someone who became involved with the occult, had a bad experience and came away. But I wanted to be sure that everyone knew that this was the *wrong* thing to do. So I changed it to mean that if anyone found themselves in the company of this kind of being, they'd better get out of there fast, stay away, beware the Devil Woman.

I once received a letter from a girl in Australia who was about to get involved with the occult when a friend of hers said, 'You're a Cliff Richard fan, play this.' She listened to the record and wrote to me saying, 'I did not get involved and I'm now a member of a church in Melbourne.' I couldn't believe it! That was just a pop song. It doesn't mention Jesus at all, but he used it. It sold a few million but it *could* have been recorded just for her.

Over the years, there has been the difficulty of media attention, but I can't see any way round that. I went to watch Kenneth Branagh during the filming of *Hamlet* with Derek Jacobi, when I was planning my show *Heathcliffe*. Kenneth asked how it was going and I replied, 'I'm finding it so *difficult* that the press have already slated the show and we haven't even got a script yet. It's just the idea of it. I wish I could grow a thick skin that was impervious to all these things.' And he said, 'Don't wish it upon yourself. The reason why *we* do what we do is *because* our skin is thin. We are emotional, sensitive people and it's always going to be painful, but don't wish for a thick skin.' That has made it much easier for me although it's not comfortable to read things about yourself that have been fabricated or deliberately misrepresented. The press don't always lie, but they lie by *omission*. If they are given a sentence, one part being a statement and another part qualifying what has been said, they leave off the qualifying factor, and you sound like an arrogant dictator of other people's thoughts. That's always going to be painful. But I remembered what Branagh had said and thought if it *really hurts*, it means that I'm still sensitive.

When TEAR Fund (The Evangelical Alliance Relief Fund) entered my life, it played a major role in my Christian maturity. Until then I could theorise about what I could do for others, but had no means by which I could actually *do* it. And it's too easy, if you have money, to give some of it away. It's something that can be done to salve the conscience. TEAR Fund helped me get out to the places where I could actually see for myself what pain and suffering people go through, and it motivated me increasingly to be involved with them. I do pray for 'the world', but don't expect God to actually 'zap' the planet so that it will evolve differently with freedom from all poverty and pain, although I believe that's going to happen at some point. He wants us to play the major role. It would be all too easy for God to 'zap' it and then we would have done nothing. But in the meantime we're left wondering about the suffering, wondering about earthquakes, wondering about why people die of curable diseases and still questioning, 'God, why don't you just "zap" the ones that need it!'

It's too easy, if you have money

My first visit with TEAR Fund was in 1973. In the hospital in Bangladesh most people were dying of curable illnesses like TB, and they only had five nurses from Britain to deal with 500 beds. They were an unbelievable group of young women and to me they were the spearhead of what Christianity is about. That was Jesus in action and to anyone who says God doesn't care for these people, I would reply 'Why does he send these girls there?' The nurses said, 'We know God loves these people because we are here. Although we said, yes, we'll come, he sent us here, he made us aware of what we have to do.'

As a Christian, I feel that I don't always succeed. I can't emulate Jesus well enough to say I've achieved perfection! We all aim at that, but we can't do it. Conflict is constantly there, and where my career has controlled me, it's because I've let it control me. Sometimes one is in danger of believing the fantasy of the general persona that you become when you are a 'celebrity'. You can't help it sometimes of course, when people are screaming after you and shouting for your autograph, but I feel I've somehow managed to control that side of my career.

In terms of my faith, I've struggled like everyone does, I suppose, in keeping up with it. I've forced myself, and I use the word advisedly, to read the Bible. I don't always want to read it but I've said to myself, 'If I'm not going to stay static or even drop backwards, I have to continue to take in some information.' I don't study it but everyday I read a chapter from the Bible and use Daily Light. And sometimes I am really eager to read and pray.

The biggest challenge is trying to imitate Jesus. In our daily lives as Christians he is the only role model. Jesus means the future for me. There is no Millennium without him. He was the beginning of everything and he'll be the end of everything. I consider myself to be most fortunate to have heard of him and to have met people who were prepared to share him with me. And so, my life is dependent upon Jesus, not just the life I have now, but also my future. I think those of us who have accepted Jesus have accepted heaven. We don't even deserve it. There's nothing we can do to earn it. He gives it to us if we ask. And therefore, Jesus means everything to me. He is my raison d'être.

Sometimes one is in danger of believing the fantasy

MAX LUCADO

IT ALL BEGAN WITH ONE MAN

I trace my spiritual birth back to an event soon after I graduated from high school in 1973. I had been raised in a Christian home, made an early profession of faith and was baptised as a ten-year-old, but I believe that I embraced the faith later on and for me the turning point was one summer night when I was eighteen years old.

I grew up in West Texas, honest-to-goodness cowboy country; most of the people wore boots and jeans. Some parts of Texas pretend to look cowboy but these were real ranchers. My good friend James was raised on a ranch and my father was in the oil business. We used to get drunk every weekend; that's how we had our fun; we saved up our money all week and bought a case of beer at the weekend. I knew it wasn't right, because when doing that, other things aren't right too, like running with the wrong kind of people. Life isn't going anywhere.

One particular summer's night in July 1973 James and I were sitting in his pickup truck in front of a grocery store in our small West Texas town watching the cars drive up and down the main street. We were drinking beer and although I had drunk six beers, I didn't feel anything. With time, the more a person drinks the more alcohol it takes to get him drunk and I realised what was happening to me. I was becoming a drunk. I had reached the point where I could drink a whole six-pack and not feel anything. I turned to James and said 'There's got to be more to life than this.' I don't remember what he said and I don't remember what I said after that, but in my heart, I made a decision: 'I'm not going to live my life like this. If God will take me back, I'm going to go home to God.' What's strange is that although that marked the beginning of the journey it still took me another two years to make the full commitment to Christ. I went on to college and I did stop drinking and I did stop running around with that bad crowd, but I still didn't understand why Jesus died on the cross, and I still didn't understand his love for me until the spring of my sophomore year in College.

I attended a special revival meeting at the church and the preacher made it so clear that I was probably the first one down the aisle to *rededicate* my life to Christ. What held me back during that two-year period — and I know it's an excuse that I hear myself today — but there are so many people who called themselves Christians but didn't practise their faith. In my heart I was saying 'I'm going to wait 'till I'm really *ready* to give my life to God', and I was ready. I discovered that I could not save myself. I didn't understand grace, even though I'd been raised in a church. I thought the more good things I did, the more chance I had of going to heaven, which is contrary to the gospel of grace. And it wasn't that no one had explained it to me, it was just that I wasn't listening. I couldn't embrace 'Blessed are the *poor* in spirit for theirs is the kingdom of heaven'; I still felt 'blessed are the *affluent* in good works'. I thought there was something to be said about doing all these good works and now I understood that we do good works, not to be saved but because we *are* saved. With that realisation I said, 'OK — I can relax!' And I did, and I stopped trying to earn my way. I'm still learning that. I think that's a life-long process.

About six months later I had an invitation to go and spend the summer in Brazil working with missionaries. I went with some friends and we built fences at a Christian camp. It wasn't anything sophisticated but it was enough to impress me with the importance of working in

> **There's got to be more to life than this**

mission fields and working as a missionary. I decided then that this should my future. In those days, to get into Brazil as a missionary a degree in theology was necessary so I had to stay on at college and get a Masters degree in theology. I took a course in preaching and this created a new interest. I returned to Brazil with a new-found love for preaching and, as a way to relax while studying the language, I wrote a journal in English to take my mind off Portuguese. That was when I started writing. Some friends said 'You ought to try to get this published.' So I tried. It took me fifteen attempts but finally it was accepted. God's way of getting me into what I do now, preaching and writing, was by sending me to Brazil.

The preparation to get into Brazil got me interested in preaching and the study of the Portuguese language got me interested in writing. I never set out to write. I never thought I would preach, but here I am and it all started in a pickup truck drinking beer.

I started as pastor of Oak Hills Church of Christ in San Antonio in 1988. I hope that this is a place where, if God is looking for a church where he can say every week 'I love you' he will do it here. I believe that each church has its theme message based on the ministry of the pastor. Our theme message is 'God loves you right where you are. He doesn't want to leave you there. He wants you to be just like Jesus. But He loves you right where you are.' And there's nothing we can ever do to make him love us more or to diminish his love. It's out of that *love* and out of that understanding that we begin our journey with Christ.

We have in our church many recovering legalists. And that's probably because I am one. If I was a former prison inmate maybe we'd have a lot of former prison inmates. Because I understand what it's like to try to earn a way to heaven, God brings us people who are coming out of legalistic churches where they've been taught that they have to do this and that, and *hope* they go to heaven. They never have any assurance, but just *hope* that they'll get there. One of the most dramatic conversions is the conversion from Saul to Paul, the conversion on the road to Damascus of a legalist who is discovering grace. We have a lot of that here and once those people are set free, they're excited! It's liberation!

When I write I take my books out of my sermons; I will preach it to the church first. One series called 'Travelling Light' is based on the 23rd Psalm — the thesis is that we all carry burdens we're not supposed to carry. Every morning we get up, go to the baggage claim, and pick up some bags that God doesn't want us to carry. The 23rd Psalm reminds us of all the bags we're supposed to leave alone. The Lord is my Shepherd. There's the bag of self-sufficiency . . . I have to do it all myself. I'm in charge of the universe. But God says, 'Leave that bag alone and let me be your shepherd. Let me lead you, let me feed you, let me guide you.' We study that for a few months and then I'll sit down with it over a couple of weeks and try to put it into book form.

I preach sermons on 'Travelling Light' because I need to remember the Lord is my shepherd. I really try to give my struggles to God and the one thing that helps me is to endeavour to live in a constant sense of God's presence. I'm trying to get my thought process to the stage where every few minutes I say, 'God, I know you're here,' or 'God, I'm giving this to you' or 'God, forgive me,' and so live in a state of communion.

I have two places where I do my writing — we have a small house on a lake about two hours from here, and the other is in my church office. When I'm writing I feel extremely focused. God has *not* given me the ability to think about a lot of things at one time but he has given me the ability to think about *one* thing very intently. I can lock into a project and focus on that book or chapter or whatever needs to be written that day and not think about anything for about eight or ten hours at a time. It's a wonderful gift and enables me to accomplish things.

> . . . that's
> probably because
> I am one

The bad news is that I forget everything else. If I have to mail some bills or call somebody, I don't even think about it. It's almost like submerging in a project, I don't come up for air until I feel like it and then I get lost again. It's not effortless, it's just not painful. I believe that when a person becomes a Christian, God gives them a spiritual gift. A talent is something that is received at physical birth; a gift is something received at spiritual birth. And sometimes God will take a talent and turn it into a spiritual gift, and sometimes he won't. But a spiritual gift is used to advance the kingdom of God. A person might have a talent for singing, but when they sing, if *others* don't think about God, it's not a gift. And believe me, when I sing, others won't think about God! But if I have a gift, when I sing, it will make people want to draw closer to God. My voice may not be spectacular or a sermon might not be that breathtaking, but because God anoints it, it will make a difference. I believe every Christian has a gift, and when we put that gift to work, it's wonderful. It's like the difference between stairs and escalators. There's still a little bit of effort but sometimes it is possible to stand still and still move up.

I always say the best decisions I ever made were to follow Christ and to marry Denalyn; she's just a delight! We went to the same college but didn't date and we ended up in Miami, Florida, on the way to Brazil. I stopped in Miami to preach and work at a church for two years while the rest of the team going to Brazil with me were finishing their education. Denalyn moved there to teach at a school, we fell in love, got married and we now have three lovely daughters. I try to leave my evenings free, which is different. A lot of pastors fill their evenings up. I have one evening a week, which is committed, but the others I try to leave free to be at home. I find that my energy is restored when I'm at home and I just love being with my family.

I love exercise and enjoy watching sports and I was thinking recently that the hardest thing in my life is hitting a golf ball. God's been so *good* to me, the church is growing, the family's healthy and I've got more ideas for books than I've time to write. Our plan and our prayer is to be here for our whole life; we'd like to make Oak Hills a lifework. However, by the time this goes to press, I may be in another city, maybe back in Brazil. It's just a good time in our life and I realise that God could change that tomorrow. The pain of maturity may come, but right now it's a very good season.

One thing that occurred to me as I considered the new Millennium is that half the world is different because of Christ in these last 2,000 years. It's really different. Can you imagine how the world would be if it wasn't for Christ? And it all began with one man in that small country. In Matthew Chapter 28 the angel said, 'He is not here. He is risen, just as he said he would.' And I thought how those words changed the world. It has never been the same and for 2,000 years now we have been able to live with the *hope of resurrection*. This isn't the end: it's like somebody burrowing a tunnel and suddenly bursting through the dirt wall and realising they've got all the way through the mountain. Instead of just walking into a dark cave, we walk through a tunnel and that's what life is.

Before Christ, life was a cave, once into it there wasn't a way out; it was dark. But Christ, when he came, burrowed all the way through and light now comes at us from the other side of the tunnel.

> ## I believe
> ## every Christian
> ## has a gift

It was 1969. I could hear the clank, clank, clank of the milk being delivered in the cans one morning at 4.00 am. I looked up into the sky and saw a comet. It was awesome!!!!

It is hard to describe but the head and then the tail sprawling more than twenty full moons was visible. It was an incredible spectacle to behold. I immediately rushed out with a 400 ASA film, put my little Canon camera on a tripod, and photographed it. I later showed my father and told him 'This is Comet Bennett. I'd love to know more.' He asked who Bennett was. I said, 'Well, on the radio they said that he's a South African astronomer.' My dad suggested I go and visit him. I said, 'Dad, I can't. I'm a schoolboy. How can I go and speak to this great astronomer?' But my Dad persisted, 'David, all he can do is say no, or he's too busy.' So I phoned him in Pretoria and said, 'Sir, it's a great honour to be speaking to you. I'd just like to know if I could possibly come over and meet with you and perhaps you could tell me what a comet is. It's certainly an incredibly beautiful object you've discovered.' And he replied, 'David, come!'

I was so inspired when I met him. Soon after that, the great British astronomer Patrick Moore was in South Africa; his BBC television programme was *The Sky At Night*. He was speaking at the Wits Planetarium in Johannesburg and afterwards when I went up to him he handed me his card. That was a very special moment, and he said, 'If there are any questions you ever have on astronomy, give me a call.' I remember sending him some photographs I had taken and he responded.

Looking back, I think it was the great personal interest that Jack Bennett and Patrick Moore took in my life, which really served as the great catalyst to start me on the road of astronomy.

I was born into an orthodox Jewish family on 16 February 1954, in Krugersdorp in South Africa. It has been a tremendous privilege to go to the synagogue and hear great rabbinical sermons about God speaking to Abraham, Isaac, Jacob, but somehow God was very far removed from me. He was the God of the Bible. He was the God who existed in these people's minds, but certainly didn't exist today.

I will never forget travelling to London and visiting Patrick Moore. We went to a meeting of the Royal Astronomical Society, in Burlington House, Piccadilly. It was great! We had the world's grandest astronomers and cosmologists there including Stephen Hawking. However, when I went back to my hotel room that night, I felt so alone even though there were throngs of people in London. My room was very dark, and certainly it was very lonely. I didn't know the God in the Bible of whom King David said: 'He is my Shepherd.' I didn't know him.

As a schoolboy, I was depressed at times just thinking of the awesomeness of the cosmos but what really made me despondent was death. There was definitely the sense of meaninglessness that Shakespeare writes about — 'like a player strutting on the stage, and then it is past.'

In 1972, I entered University of the Witwatersrand and started studying for my BSc degree. The more I studied astronomy, the more I became aware of the beauty in the night sky but it seemed as if there was no link between the God of the Bible and my personal experience. There was no link at all.

One day a family friend, Lewis Hurst, a professor of Genetics and Medicine, asked if I would mind giving him lessons on astronomy. We met on a weekly basis and I taught him about

I will never forget travelling to London and visiting Patrick Moore

the cosmos, the expanding universe, black holes and time in relativity. I remember saying to Lewis, 'The cosmos really is beautiful, but it's so big. We live seventy years or so and we pass away. Somehow, Prof, there's just no meaning to the cosmos that I'm teaching you about.' And he replied, 'Oh, there is. I know you come from an orthodox Jewish background but would you agree to meet a friend of mine?' I asked who the friend was and he said, 'He's a minister, the Rev John Spyker.' I agreed to meet him.

We went to his home; he looked me in the eye when I walked into his room and said, 'When I think of the evangelistic work that you are going to do, my blood runs cold!' Well, I didn't know what he meant by that! We chatted and then he said, 'There is only one verse in the Bible that I'd like to read for you.' He opened his Bible and read from Romans 9:33, 'Behold, I lay in Zion a stumblingstone and rock of offence: and whosoever believeth on him shall not be ashamed.' Suddenly, as a Jew, I knew that 'the rock of offence' was Jesus. And I said, 'Pray for me.'

I had been fasting every Yom Kippur, The Day of Atonement, 'May my sins be forgiven', but I had no assurance that they were forgiven or that God was real. The Rev Spyker prayed with me and I not only made a commitment to follow Jesus but something far more important happened. I experienced a wonderful warmth flowing through my body, and the Spirit of God entered me. What was so wonderful was that his personality became so vibrant in my life, much like, I suppose, the Ethiopian Eunuch on the chariot, who went on his way, rejoicing!

When I accepted Jesus my father said, 'I can see changes in you and it's wonderful, but just keep it quiet.' I was simply a university student and wasn't by any means a well-known figure at that stage, but he said, 'Please keep it quiet because as a Jew, all hell's going to break loose if you speak about the Jewish Messiah.'

I went public with my faith anyway and, as my father had told me, all hell did indeed break loose. The rabbis wanted him to hold a burial service for me to proclaim me dead. Then, if they passed me in the street, they wouldn't greet me because you don't greet a dead person! There was a tremendous amount of flak behind the scenes as far as my father and mother were concerned but they didn't go through with the service. By having accepted Jesus, I felt so much more Jewish than I ever felt before.

Since then I have spoken to large crowds, been on television with Pat Robinson and spoken for Lauren Cunningham in Hawaii. What I think has been so wonderful is that I have never left being a Professor of Applied Maths and Astronomy. Many people believe that in order to be an effective Christian it is necessary to give up the use of your brain and somehow deprive yourself of creativity, but that is so far removed from the work of God that I see in front of my eyes. The Creator of the starry skies. A Creative God! A God who loves making corals under the sea, who loves making a flower, who makes us unique and irreplaceable.

When I reflect on Sir Isaac Newton who was deeply aware of the Creator, and Pascal who had a profound conversion experience with Jesus, it became clear, very early on, that I should not give up my calling as an academic. I was elected a Fellow of the Royal Astronomical Society at the age of nineteen and had my first paper published at the age of twenty. I gained a Masters Degree in Relativistic Astrophysics and my Doctorate in the Morphology (which is the shapes) of Spiral Galaxies.

A highlight of my research career was to lead a team who *conclusively* proved the existence of cold and very cold cosmic dust grains in other galaxies. And by cold, I mean *very* cold, dust grains at temperatures of around $-250°$ C. By using special detectors to remove the dust curtain, we were able to look through the cosmic dust veil to the galaxies.

The rabbis wanted him to hold a burial service for me

Subsequently I was told, and I take this with a tremendous sense of humility, that I am one of the few scientists in the world whose research has twice been featured on the cover of the journal *Nature*. I ask, 'God, Why?' I suppose it is his own way of saying, 'David, look up!' It was hard growing up and as a schoolboy I always used to look down so much. Somehow, I think that these are 'kisses of love' from the Father.

I started lecturing and working on my PhD at the University of Cape Town and felt the need for a companion. I thought it would be wonderful to share my Christian experience with somebody else and yet that somebody else was not forthcoming. I started giving slide presentations at churches entitled 'The Heavens Declare the Glory of God', and I used to meet lots of different people, but there was no meeting with my wife.

My parents would have loved me to marry a Jewish girl, for many reasons, but I suppose the biggest reason was, TRADITION! Fiddler on the Roof! Tradition! They could see the change in my life and I'm sure that in the back of their minds they really hoped David would come to his senses and marry a nice Jewish girl!

I remember asking God at one stage, 'Lord, where is my wife? What sort of wife should I pray for?' He said, 'A Jewish girl who loves Jesus!' Now in retrospect, that is a far harder prayer to pray than I could ever have thought. While I am sure there are a lot of Jewish people who might *secretly* be believers in Jesus the Messiah, I do realise that the number of Jewish people who openly come out and say, 'Jesus is the Jewish Messiah' is very small. In Cape Town there were many *krugels*, young Jewish girls, but I wasn't finding my wife. And when I told God this, in a sense he simply seemed to say, 'It's because you are begging me.' And he reminded me of Matthew 17:20, 'If you have faith as small as a mustard seed, you can say to this mountain, "Move from here to there" and it will move. Nothing will be impossible for you.'

I received a telegram inviting me to be the Senior Lecturer in Astronomy at the University of The Orange Free State. That couldn't have been a greater shock to me because the Free State is very small and the Jewish population could be numbered on a couple of hands. Bloemfontein didn't turn me on at all, but I moved anyway!

I couldn't find accommodation and was staying with a minister for a few days. He informed me, 'There's a widow who has got a huge home, rather like a farm, and she's looking for a boarder, a respectable gentleman who doesn't make too much noise and doesn't party too much.' It was a very large home, large enough to hold classical concerts in it!

After attending one such concert I went outside to join in a wonderful meal that was being served. A woman came up and asked me if I was David Block. When I said yes, she replied, 'Hi, I'm Liz Levitt and I just wanted to introduce myself. I heard you were coming to town.' Levitt — that's from the tribe of Levi — more kosher you really can't get! We started chatting, and eventually we were married in Bloemfontein!

It's so wonderful, when I look back now, that I met a Jewess as my parents wanted, but more than that, I got someone who really loves Jesus. Liz is on the board of Jews for Jesus, South Africa, and is an extremely interesting personality. She lectures in Soweto and was one of the few whites willing to travel there in the 1980s when armoured tanks patrolled the streets.

After nine years of marriage Liz and I had probably resigned ourselves to the fact that we wouldn't have children — when Aaron was conceived. He is an absolute joy and is just wonderful. Six years later our twin boys Tevye and Nathanael were born, so the message I now give to childless people is, 'Don't give up!' I think that God was smiling on us when he gave us our twins, to whom President Mandela has given Xhosa names: Nkwenkwezi, which means 'star', and Khethile 'the chosen one'.

These are 'kisses of love'

God has so many surprises in store for each of us. As I look back over my career, it has been wonderful to have been the author of *Star Watch*, and a great encouragement to have two Nobel Prize winners endorse my book, *Our Universe – Accident or Design?* In one endorsement the Nobel Prize winner in Physics, Arno Penzias says, 'Astronomy leads us to a unique event. A universe, which was created out of nothing and delicately balanced to provide exactly the conditions required to support life. In the absence of an absurdly improbable accident, the observations of modern science seem to suggest an underlying, one might say supernatural, plan.' To think that a Nobel Prize winner in Physics is saying that the observations of modern astronomy point to a Creator is *absolutely awesome.*

When I think of the way 15,000 million years ago, God used an incredibly finely-tuned recipe to create this cosmos, then I can again start appreciating the statement in John 1: 'In the beginning was the Word, and the Word was with God, and the Word was God.' There's a lovely quote by James Trefil that pertains to all of this, '. . . But we are living on an insignificant speck of rock going round an undistinguished star in a low-rent section of the galaxy. We are not the centre of the universe. *Maybe so, but we are special.* But we share our biochemistry with millions of life forms from flat worms up. We are one member of a large family of animals using one particular variant of carbon chemistry known as DNA. *Maybe so, but we are special.* Why? Because only on this insignificant speck of rock have beings evolved who can look at the universe and ask the question: Why?!' That's really it. We are self-aware human beings who can ask 'why' questions. And I think it's so wonderful that certainly, in my domain of astronomy, as I ask why, I can get the answer, 'David, I'm here!'

Why are you so excited about cosmic dust?

I am exceedingly proud to be a scientist who is a Christian. I am deeply moved and challenged to be able to represent my Lord in the highly competitive field of astronomy. A lot of my research has been on cosmic dust, on probing cosmic dust. People ask me, 'Why are you so excited about cosmic dust, David?' Well, what did God make us from? Dust!

I can tell you about this cosmic dust but what is so important, is that God, who made a hundred thousand million stars in our Milky Way galaxy alone, somehow is the God who I can say is my Shepherd. He cares for me and has given me a message to tell people worldwide, 'Look up. Never give up.'

In Psalm 147 we read, 'He heals the brokenhearted and binds up their wounds. He determines the number of the stars and calls them each by name.' That's awesome. A hundred thousand million stars and he calls them all by name! And yet, he cares enough to heal our broken hearts and bind up our wounds!!!!

I was raised in the mountains of Western North Carolina. As a young person I was probably more under the influence of my mother — she raised us as children — Daddy was gone a considerable amount of time and so she was the disciplinarian. My mother was a student of the Scriptures and knows the Bible backwards and forwards. She applied it to her walk in life and was never stuffy in her faith. Her faith was alive, it was real, and she'd made it exciting. So, when we were little she made our house fun to live in.

It was, in some respects, like a single parent home but when Daddy came home he certainly tried his best to make up for his absence. He was always bigger than life to us children, somebody we admired and loved. When I needed him he would always stop whatever he was doing and make time for me. He was gone sometimes two, three, even up to six months at a time.

His ministry started right after the Second World War. Soldiers had been away from home for five years fighting for the defence of freedom and had paid a huge price and he felt they could do no less for the preaching of the gospel. I think if he had to do it today, he wouldn't do it that way, nevertheless that's the way they did it in those years, and I don't think I was deprived.

On one particular day there was a rattlesnake . . .

My mother had an unbelievable amount of energy and has a great sense of humour. We had poisonous snakes all around our home and one year we killed seventy. When we would go out walking, we would always carry either a gun or a big stick. Rattlesnakes are very poisonous, not to be messed with, because they can actually jump twice the length of their body, so if one is 6 feet long and coiled up, he can jump up to about 12 feet!

On one particular day there was a rattlesnake that Mama thought it would be fun to catch. We had what we called a marshmallow fork with which she wanted to pin the head so she could reach down and pick it up. The snake saw Mama coming with that big fork and it decided to leave. It slithered down the side of the mountain with Mama right on its tail, trying to poke it. We were yelling and screaming, 'Mama, get away from the snake.' She followed that thing all the way down and finally the snake got away from her.

When I got married she had one of the caretakers put a little, non-poisonous garden snake inside my suitcase. On my honeymoon, when I would open up my suitcase to get my clothes out, that snake would be a source of entertainment, I guess! But a friend, who did not know about this, broke into the case to remove my underwear, thinking it would be funny for me to go on my honeymoon with no underwear. On opening the suitcase up popped the snake and, of course, it scared him. He slammed the suitcase shut but didn't know he'd caught the snake's head. The snake slithered down to the bottom of my suitcase and died. About three or four days later . . . my clothes! Was it I, or did my deodorant not work, or something? But she did things like that. A lot of fun.

My parents loved me but no matter how much they cared they could not choose Jesus Christ for me. Even though our family comes out of strong Presbyterian roots, that was a choice I had to make. My mother was raised in a Presbyterian home as was my father. Many people think he was raised Baptist, but reformed theology is his background. But they knew, and I knew, that I was going to have to make a choice and so, in my teenage years I did not want God in my life.

FRANKLIN GRAHAM

To my surprise
my father agreed

I wanted to make my own way, I wanted to find those things that would make me happy, that would please me, that would serve my interests, and giving my life to Jesus Christ, surrendering my life to someone else sounded pretty boring. I think many people resist coming to Christ because they feel they don't want anyone to control their destiny.

I'm a product of my generation — the sixties, early-seventies, raised on rock and roll, the influence of the Beatles, Elvis Presley and those types of people. I rebelled against authority; I rebelled against the establishment. But more than anything, I rebelled against God. I didn't want controls in my life. I didn't want someone telling me I could not do this or that. I wanted freedom because I thought it would bring happiness, peace and joy but there was an emptiness that came instead. And no matter what I tried, there was still emptiness. You search when you don't know you're searching. You're looking when you don't even realise you're looking. I think that's why people use drugs and alcohol; I think that's why people get hooked on pornography and sex.

While I was searching in the early-seventies, I went to work in a little mission hospital in Northern Jordan out in the desert, a little place called Mafraq, about thirty miles south of the Syrian border. Jordan had just gone through a small civil war called Black September, where the Palestinians tried to overthrow King Hussein and he put them down — it was pretty bloody. It is said that he took 20,000 into the desert, threw them out of the trucks and left them to make their own way back; most of them died in the desert. I heard of two ladies who had a little mission hospital and needed a Land Rover because the Palestinians had stolen their car. I wanted some adventure and excitement but knew I needed a good evangelical-sounding excuse for my father and mother to agree to let me drop out of school!

I didn't enjoy school. I enjoyed the outdoors and the openness of the woods. I never liked the confinements of a classroom and I think maybe that's why I like to fly aeroplanes — the openness of the sky and the freedom of the wind. I told the ladies I had been praying about being a missionary and that I wanted to go to help them in the mission hospital for several months to gain experience. To my surprise, my father agreed. So I said, 'Well, Dad, I need you to buy the Land Rover!' And again he agreed.

He called the lady in charge of the London office and told her to purchase a Land Rover. She returned his call, 'Dr Graham, you just don't go buying a Land Rover. These things are specially built. There's a waiting list for them and right now, there are none for sale.' However, on my father's suggestion she called the factory, to be told 'Yes, we do have *one* that's available. It was built for a client in the Middle East. It does not have a heater but it has been double sealed for sand, and if you would like that one, you can buy it, but that's the only one we have.' She replied, 'That's exactly what we're looking for!' And so I drove it from London to the Middle East, to Jordan.

After finishing my work at the mission, I went back to college for two years, graduating in May 1974 when I left for Switzerland to help the BGEA at the Lausanne conference. At night sometimes there wasn't anything to do so I just started reading my New Testament. As I began to read, I believe that God started to convict me of my sin.

In July, on my 22nd birthday my father said, 'Franklin, I would like to take you out for dinner to celebrate.' 'Great,' I thought, and picked a little Italian restaurant down by Lake Geneva. After dinner he said, 'Franklin, I'd like to talk to you. I want you to know that your mother and I love you very much and the door at home will always be open to you.' I sensed he wanted to say something else but he was slow getting around to it. Finally he stopped, just looked at me and said, 'Franklin, I sense that there is a struggle for the soul of your life and you're going to have to choose either to accept Christ or to reject him. There *is* no middle ground. You cannot ride the fence on this one and I want you to know that your mother and I are praying that you'll make the right decision.' I felt as if I had been struck with a knife. It made me mad, but that conversation was the key that began to unlock my heart.

About two weeks later, in Jerusalem, I realised that I was lost, that I was a sinner, that there was an emptiness in my life and that I had a vacuum which could only be filled by a right relationship with Almighty God.

I read the Scripture and getting on my knees said, 'God, if you are who you are and your Son Jesus Christ is who you claim he is, I want you to forgive me because I have sinned against you. I have rebelled, I have been trying to run my own life and I've made a mess of it, and if you'll take my life and put the pieces of my life back together, you can have it, it's yours. I'm sorry and I want to give Jesus Christ the control of my heart and my life from this day forward.'

At that time I was a heavy smoker and I just took my cigarettes, three or four packs, and threw them away. In the middle of the night I had bad abdominal cramps as a result of having eaten something that did not agree with me. I sat up in bed with cramps and when they subsided fell back on the pillow, but missed the pillow and hit the corner of the bedside table. I split my head wide open and must have been knocked unconscious. Of course, next morning when I woke up the sheets and the pillow were soaked in blood. I had to see a doctor to have stitches in my head. But that day I didn't even want a cigarette, my head hurt so badly. So the Lord got me through that first day without a cigarette, by hitting me on the head and knocking some sense into me, I guess!

I only smoked a cigarette once after that. It was about a week later and when I took a drag on that cigarette the taste and desire had gone. I had tried to give up on a number of occasions but never could so he actually took the desire away. I believe you can be a Christian and smoke, but I also believe nicotine, alcohol, or any other kind of drug has a control over a person. So I just thank God that he freed me from that control. Christ came into my heart and changed my life.

On 14th August 1974 I married Jane Austin whom I'd known most of my life. We started dating when I was eighteen so we had dated for four or five years. I wasn't sure after that what I should do. I'd been out of school for a while and decided to go back to finish my education, took a degree in business and came to Boone, North Carolina, to study business at university — over twenty years later I'm still here.

Bob Pierce, one of the early founders of Youth for Christ, really was the father of evangelical compassion and brought to light the need for relief-type ministries. George Hoffman followed him in the UK with TEAR Fund and it was my privilege to know and work with both these men.

Bob had leukaemia and one day said, 'Franklin, I'd like you to take over Samaritan's Purse.' It was located in Hollywood and I told him, 'Bob, I love the work you do, I love the ministry of helping people but I don't want to live in California.' He replied, 'I don't care where you live. You can move it to North Carolina. But I can't choose my successor, Franklin, my Board of Directors are going to have to make that choice.' About four days after that he died.

A year later the Board made their choice: 'Franklin, we think you should be there.' And I accepted. We kept the office in Hollywood for the first year and then moved it to North Carolina. There were only four or five of us then — we weren't very big — but over the years it has grown into a much larger organisation.

I felt as if I had been struck with a knife

At Samaritan's Purse we look for areas of crisis, war and famine where we can help people. I feel that if a person is down in the ditch of life's circumstances, for whatever reason, if you stop and help him, he's going to listen to what you have to say and it gives us a chance to present the gospel. Some people feel that's taking advantage of people when they are weak. But I'm not at them for what I can gain for myself. I will however, take advantage of every opportunity to communicate the truth. If that person is dying and on their way to hell, and I give them water, food and clothes but don't warn them about what's lying ahead, then their blood would be on my hands. We want to use every opportunity in life to present the gospel. I've spent the last twenty-seven years building a business, not for myself, I don't have any stock in. I can't sell it or trade it because it's the Lord's business.

Telling men and women about God's Son, the Lord Jesus Christ, who came to this earth to die for the sins of this world, that he's alive and is going to come back some day, is at the heart of everything we want to do. I want people to know that God *will* forgive their sin but they have to come to God in a very specific way and it's through Jesus Christ — 'Jesus [said] "I am the way and the truth and the life. No-one comes to the Father except through me."' That is our heart — to proclaim the gospel. We do humanitarian work but we're an evangelistic organisation. We don't hide it, we don't apologise for it, and we make it very clear in everything we do. We're here to win people for Christ. And we don't compromise that. We *will not* compromise that.

We don't hide it, we don't apologise for it

DANIEL RUFFINATTI
HE SAVED ME FROM FIRE

Born in Buenos Aires, Argentina, in 1956, I was brought up in a home where all the traditions and activities of the local church were respected. I went to Sunday School where I learnt a lot about the Bible, but my childhood was not very happy because my parents quarrelled a lot. At ten years old, in an emotional public meeting, a preacher called the people to make a commitment, and I raised my hand and said that I accepted Jesus Christ.

The idea was to create a force similar to the SS

Two years later at twelve, I was baptised in water and from that moment, my participation in church became very important. I sang in the choir and sometimes preached to the young people. I went out with them to distribute Christian literature door-to-door but something was happening in my life that was not visible to others. I was creating a double life. Everybody in church regarded me as spiritually good because I always attended the services, had my hair cut in a traditional style and wore normal clothing. On Sunday my life was holy but I was similar to a coffin, very nice on the outside but ugly inside! This inner life was growing and it led me into disobedience and a lot of sexual encounters.

After High School I went to seminary for one year. I met and fell in love with a girl but there was opposition from her family so we ran far away from Buenos Aries. I knew about praying but I did not apply it when I made the decision to leave the seminary. Shortly after the girl became pregnant and from then on life was very difficult. I went to medical school but had to leave before I completed my second year. My secular career was incomplete, we couldn't find any work and lived in very poor conditions.

We decided to go back to Buenos Aires and let our parents help us, a decision born of necessity, not real change. I tried to go back to church but felt I was worshipping God with my mouth and my heart was far from him. I finally found an administration job, with the Federal Police. They offered training, good medical assistance, an interesting salary and the possibility of finishing my studies so that I could work as a police doctor in the future. I had to do military training because the police were considered a military corps. When this period finished I was classified as a person suitable for a military position within the police — a special force to quell disturbances.

I tried to resign but it was impossible. Due to the political situation in Argentina in 1973/74, there was a lot of violence in the police force. Everybody was classified, with no options, and I was not allowed to change my place in the police. Most of the things we did went against what I had learned as a child. The idea was to create a force similar to the SS in the Second World War. In training we sang military songs and were not allowed to mention Jewish or communist people without including insulting language. By intimidation we were able to make a crowd of 2,000 people retreat. We learnt how to rob cars, make homemade bombs and to hate each other.

Sometimes we would guard a door, knowing that behind it people were being killed. At that time, it was common to receive a radio message in the night about a specific coloured truck containing fifty packages. Lights were turned out in the Department and when the truck arrived the fifty packages would be children and old people who were naked, perhaps bound with ropes, shaking, with cold and fear. We knew that they would disappear.

DANIEL RUFFINATTI

He had shot my friend with my gun . . .

On many occasions we had to form into groups and the people were then brought into a square in the city to be killed. Each group was given grenades and sometimes we worked for fifty hours at a time. This caused me to have violence problems so I slept late and drank a lot of alcohol. It was normal for policemen to kill themselves and most had broken families. I beat my wife and child regularly and can remember quarrelling with my sister, holding her on the floor with a gun ready to shoot her, my mother pleading with me to let her be. I lived in this violent atmosphere for around fifteen years.

I became so violent that the police eventually sent me to be checked by a medical doctor who referred me to a psychiatric doctor, and so began another stage in my life. I could no longer control the violence within me. I could not walk in the street or drive any more without feeling paranoid and persecuted.

When travelling by bus I would plan how to murder my fellow-passengers. I would have my weapon almost out of my coat and could have a person near me for an hour with my gun aimed at him. When I told the doctor about this he said I must have some leave and medication. He made a false diagnosis to protect my record for the future and so I began my psychiatric treatment. I mixed my medication with alcohol, causing me to have periods of amnesia. I met other policemen who lied about their psychiatric situation in order to carry on working and they used the negative things they had learned for their own gain. Through them I discovered robbery and realised that I could get, in ten minutes, what it took me a month to earn with the police, but the risk involved was losing my life. That didn't matter — I had found another way to continue being violent.

During the times I robbed, although I was afraid, I never thought about prison. Once I planned a robbery at a company where I worked as Police security but I couldn't do it myself because I was well known there. I found out when a lot of money was expected on site and when a friend of mine, who worked there, was going to be absent. I passed this information on to an accomplice and gave him my weapon. We went downtown to the company; I waited outside in the car, but something went wrong. My friend who was supposed to be absent from work had in fact gone in. It was a successful robbery but there was a shootout, and as we raced away my accomplice told me that he had shot my friend with my gun and the special bullets I had prepared for maximum damage. That night the company telephoned me and asked me to try to find out who had robbed them. As a policeman I was the first to go to the hospital to see my friend. I heard all the comments about the event, knowing all the time it was I who was responsible.

Several days later, my friend died. It was terrible. It fuelled my mental illness and sometimes, even today, when I pass by that place I remember . . .

In early 1980 I was arrested for thirteen federal crimes and twenty-four counts of armed robbery. I was taken to a large prison where I spent many days in very small cells. My cellmates and I were badly treated but I survived. Later that year I was transferred to a psychiatric prison, where the one hundred most dangerous people in the country were kept. For nearly a year I was in a square cell, the only clothing I wore being a straight jacket, and I can still remember black boots kicking me on the floor. On that floor we had to attend to our basic needs and they even put my food there.

Many prisoners killed themselves in those cellblocks. They scratched messages in the walls in which they begged God's forgiveness, and that of their mothers. Eventually I lost contact with reality. Each day I was injected and took about forty pills. At one time I did not even recognise my own mother and didn't know whether it was night or day.

It seemed as if my previous life had never been and that I had been born in this place. Everything was grey or white and colours were just a faint memory. Many who became my friends had been in that place for forty years and didn't know women existed. During this time my wife abandoned me for another man. I only saw my two children very occasionally — they were too little — and on the few occasions I saw them I had to wear a straight jacket and be behind bars. Although they were brought close to me, I wasn't allowed to touch them because they said I was too dangerous. Throughout all these terrible things, I still ignored God.

In that place the only way to survive was to team up with someone. I became friends with a Satanist who had a Bible; all the things that had a connection with the devil were underlined. He had made a twenty-day plan to read the Bible at fifty-eight pages a day. He was unable to read because his excessive medication had caused eye problems. I was able to read however, and that was how I came to read the Bible. On our fourth day, we read Deuteronomy Chapter 30. It is the chapter where God tells the Israelites that he is close by and there was no need to go far to see him. He told the people 'This day . . . I have set before you life and death, blessings and curses' and several times he said, 'Today, choose life, so you can live.' We felt God was talking and that he was there with us. We both were weeping. The next day my friend told me that he felt nothing and didn't want to touch the Bible again so I had to finish it alone.

When I finished my reading, I felt enormous happiness inside me and wondered whether it was from God or the effect of my medication. For the first time I prayed in that place and said, 'God, I know nobody is going to believe this but I'm lowering my resistance and asking for your help.' I told God that if this was truly from him, I could not speak to people about his freedom if I was still a slave to violence, drugs or crime so I asked him to liberate me from all these things. That was on 1st April 1982 and since that moment God has given me total freedom. I came off drugs without all the withdrawal symptoms, stopped smoking cigarettes, started wearing clothes and was able to communicate with other people again. Within a week seven others became Christians and a month later I started a Bible study with forty converts!

Eventually I started up a little church and it enveloped fifty per cent of the prison! We gathered every night and had several meetings in order to include everybody. The penitentiary guards, who initially regarded us very sceptically, started bringing us prayer requests, encouraging us to continue with the meetings because since starting these violence had ceased. After my personal encounter with Christ I stopped taking all medicines because I had no symptoms. Fifteen psychiatric doctors at the Law Courts where my criminal records were held had determined that I was an incurable paranoiac-schizophrenic, a danger to others and myself. I had not been criminally tried because I was judged to be mentally insane. The enormity of my crimes meant that I would be incarcerated in that place for many years. The change that Christ performed in me was so remarkable that these fifteen doctors, after checking me thoroughly for two years, released me because I had no symptoms.

In 1984 I was taken to the Hospital Borda, a psychiatric hospital, where I stayed for just over a month. The doctors there said that previous diagnoses on me must have been wrong or untrue because there was nothing wrong with me. For a while I worked as a secretary at that hospital and then I was released. For some time I had many different jobs and it took a lot for the churches to believe in me. I had the opportunity to finish my medical studies but I felt that although there were many Christian doctors, there were few who could identify with the mentally ill and be able talk to them. Six months after my release, and with support from two churches in Capital City, I started a programme in the prison where I had been an inmate, and later in the Hospital Borda.

My crimes meant that I would be incarcerated . . . for many years

These babies had no idea about freedom

Out of this programme SACDEM started and has flourished. This organisation is a Christian service for inmates and mentally ill people. The hospital board is giving assistance to fourteen hundred patients and nine federal prisons through our programme. As a result of work inside the hospital, mentally ill patients are taken on outings where they can feel the love of God and his mercy in a practical way. We take them to the SACDEM facilities where we wash and feed them. They are able to play games and we always hold services, which they really enjoy. In the prison work, our job is to make bearable the inmates' internment, to show them other possibilities and train them for a different life.

After five years of working with isolated people who had AIDS we decided to start a programme for all the children born in the prisons. SACDEM houses them permanently when they reach the age of four and have to leave prison. We felt that a text from the Bible was giving us the basis for this job. It is the Psalm that says God is the father of the orphans and defender of widows. We realised that a lot of these children were in orphan conditions and the mothers were widows. In the beginning we noticed that when I preached at meetings many of the babies that came were quiet when they heard a male voice. We could see that there were deep needs, these babies had no idea about freedom, they didn't know what a dog was, a tree, the moon, or the stars, common things for children outside the prison, so we got their mothers' authority for a recreation programme. The babies spend a week outside the prison and then return for another week with their mothers. We can do this job because of the help we receive from twenty-five Christian couples.

As time went on we realised there was another stage. Babies would stay in prison until they were four and then be sent to a government institution or be fostered out by the Courts. They lost total contact with their mothers. When a mother was released she had to have a good job, a place to live and drug rehabilitation for about a year or she had no possibility of recovering her baby. SACDEM takes responsibility for the babies' care education and twice-a-month visits with their mothers until they are released. Children live in hard situations with their biological mothers and our couples help in this area as well.

Many times I am asked questions about how things were in my life and why? I tell them a Bible story about Jesus healing the man who was blind from birth. People asked him about what had happened to him. He told them that he only knew one thing — once he was blind, and now he could see. I cannot explain the many things, either mental or spiritual, that have happened to me, but like the blind man, that has been the experience of my life. For me, Jesus is a great friend. I am a very weak person. I go wrong many times but I really feel I have a great friendship with Jesus Christ and that he gave me freedom to serve him. When I feel alone I try to open my eyes of faith, and in a tangible way I can feel that he's with me. I am the only person in Argentina who has been medically classified insane and later released, clear in mind. I have no kind of medical or psychiatric treatment now. It's quite possible because of my background, that if anyone was in need of such treatment, it ought to be me!

If I had not accepted Jesus Christ I would need that kind of treatment. I have a lot of inner hurts and scars, but I feel that God uses them to draw others to me. The doctors who released me always expect me to revert to my previous mental state because, if they say anything different, they are denying their science. The things of God are very difficult to explain. Many of the people with whom I worked in the police force, are dead or in psychiatric hospitals. It was so hard for my family but God gave me the opportunity of being with my children again. I had to tell them the truth, and the truth was that Daddy was very bad, but God forgave him and made him a new creation.

I look daily for forgiveness and understanding and have been given it. There is a Bible text that is engraved in my mind, Deuteronomy 6:12: 'Be careful that you do not forget the Lord, who brought you out of Egypt, out of the land of slavery.' I feel that God is in control and I trust him and what he has done. I have gone through some hard tests, and lots of stressful moments, but God has protected me. He saved me from fire and even, after my violent past, has put me to work with babies!

Today, after many years, my children are Christians and an example to others. I can see the many good things God has done in their lives. He also had another surprise for me. While working on a project inside the Hospital Borda, I met Maria Elena who had responded to one of my public calls for female help. I fell in love with her but didn't tell her. After some time I confessed my feelings and discovered that she was also in love with me. After praying and sharing this with our pastor, it was agreed we should marry. Maria is a wonderful wife and a perfect help in our work.

As a family, we adopted a little boy called Nicholas and are planning for ways to help all the children who will have AIDS in the future. We feel that God doesn't want an orphanage for them but rather Christian homes, which, as a result of open hearts, will be able to give them the warm love of a family. In all special cases such as terminal illness, we know that everyone who helps will suffer. The work is, in a sense, to weep with those who weep and fight for them to have a good life.

> . . . even, after my violent past, [he] has put me to work with babies!

AILEEN COLEMAN
COMPASSION FROM HIS HEART

It is very interesting that the Lord sent me to the desert where I never see the water any more! Life in my growing up years was centred on what I could do in the water, I lived for wet sports such as swimming, sailing and rowing.

I was born in Queensland, Australia, during the depression, the youngest of seven, and had a very normal, happy childhood. My parents were believers and my mother was a woman of great faith. She didn't preach at us because she didn't have to, *she lived what she believed*. My father was an accountant and although there wasn't a lot of money, he used to spend time with us on the river.

At elementary school I excelled, but in High School I scraped through because I wasn't interested in study! I hated it because it cramped my style and my sports! When I went away to nursing school I decided I had had enough of Christianity and so for the first three years I did everything available that in those days was called 'worldly'. I tried to forget the wonderful heritage I had with believing parents.

In my last year a friend dared me to go to a tent meeting saying, 'Oh, you wouldn't be game to go to that.' I knew what it was and said, 'Yea, I'm game!' And God spoke to me that night. I have never had another big crisis. I knew that Aileen Coleman's life lived for Aileen Coleman was over. Somebody pointed me to Romans 12:1 where it says, '. . . present your bodies a living sacrifice, holy, acceptable unto God, which is your reasonable service'. I love it in Arabic. It says, in translation, 'That's the common sense thing to do — to give your bodies.'

I finished my maternity training and went to Bible School not knowing what God wanted of me, but realising I needed some training in the Bible. During my second year, I was given an awful assignment on the Muslim world.

I was wild in Bible School and I think the lady superintendent thought this would keep me busy and out of trouble. In the Ladies' Residence we were all supposed to be ladies, and I wasn't! So I had the assignment on the Muslim world, which meant writing to missionaries, getting information and presenting the paper. There were few people working in the Muslim world in those days but one of the lady doctors, in what are now the Emirates in the Gulf, answered my letter. She gave me a lot of information on what they were doing and said, 'Pray that God will send us a nurse who's had postgraduate work in midwifery.' I started to pray and asked God to send them, in Arabia, a nurse who had all my qualifications.

It wasn't too long before I thought, 'This is ridiculous. I'm praying for them to find somebody that has everything I have been trained to do!' I wrote to the mission, asked them for more information and ultimately joined them.

In 1955 I went to the Gulf for a few months to replace a missionary. I became frustrated because I didn't have any Arabic and all I did was deliver babies and sleep. We were so busy and I thought, 'This isn't my idea of missionary work.' Later I was sent to Bethlehem to study Arabic, and it was there that I was asked to work in a tuberculosis hospital. At that time, we sometimes had the patients with us for years because we didn't have the medications we have today, so they had a long and loving exposure to the gospel. I started a nurses' school in that hospital and finished my language study.

I hated it because it cramped my style

AILEEN COLEMAN

Get up and do it, just start!

The missionary I went to replace got married and never came back, so I said I'd stay until they replaced me from her mission, thinking it would be a few months, but it was eight years! In that time I realised that coming to the Gulf was part of God's sovereign plan of getting me into chronic diseases as a means of evangelism with Muslim people.

I met and worked with Dr Eleanor Soltau, a tuberculosis specialist, in 1964. We soon left the hospital because we weren't really part of that mission, but we loved the work and felt, after much prayer, that we should think about moving closer to the Bedouins.

It was interesting that just before we left the hospital a man from a village about 13 km east of Mafraq, said to me, 'I hear you and the Dockturah Nor, (as they called her) are leaving this hospital. Come to our tribe, we'll give you tents to live in and a tent to put the sick people in.' To us that was our confirmation, and we went back to America, very excited, sure that it would just be wonderful and that everybody would be as excited as we were.

We were shocked and a little disappointed to see the Christian people's response. In general they were not encouraging about two women going into the Muslim world to start a hospital in what is aggressively an anti-Christian area. Several of the mission executives we talked to said, 'We'll pray for you,' which is the Christian way of sometimes saying, 'Forget it'! In Florida I visited Roy Gustafson who was then an associate evangelist with Billy Graham. He asked what we were going to do and when I told him our plans he said, 'Are you sure about this?' I was ready to get on the defensive again when he said, 'If you're so sure, what are you doing sitting here in my living room? Get up and do it, just start!' So with that Eleanor and I were encouraged. A missionary, whose father held a responsible position on the Board, agreed to channel funds. Even though they didn't agree to support the hospital, they very graciously took care of directing gifts to us.

We arrived in Mafraq in 1965, just the two of us, with very little money and two tons of equipment. Although some of it was junk there were some good things as well. A lot of the missionaries in Jordan felt the timing was wrong because of the political unrest. When we went to the Minister of Health to get permission to start many people said, 'You're not going to get a permit to start,' but people who loved us prayed when we went to see him. He listened to our requests and after what seemed like minutes, looked straight at us and said, 'Ladies, we have a *big* tuberculosis problem. Anything you can do to help us, we'll be grateful for. Where would you like to go?' When Eleanor asked where he would suggest he replied, 'Have you looked at Mafraq?'

Mafraq, meaning 'Crossroads', was a village of about 10,000 people. It was then, and still is today, a trading place where the Bedouin bring their sheep, cheese and wool to sell and barter for supplies. We went to look for a place, sure that something was there. Mafraq in those days consisted of Bedouin tents and Adobe-like mud houses, but there was a stone house in the village that we looked at and said, 'That's the place we need.'

We went back the next day and talked to the landlord. He lived on the second floor with his family, and the downstairs floor just had five rooms, but big rooms. He told us he needed a $1,000 annual rent in advance! At that time we had absolutely no money at all so we told him, 'We don't have money. Could we pay it monthly?' He replied, 'No. I need it in advance so I can start building another place, and then I'll move my family out of the second floor.' This was our first big test for finance and we did a lot of praying, purposely not asking anybody. We had two weeks' notice — if we produced the money by the end of June we could have the building. He said, 'Ah, you foreigners, you've got plenty of money!'

When Eleanor started to practise medicine in the States she had invested a small amount of money. After becoming a missionary she had never been able to save further, and so forgot all about the investment made twenty years before. On its maturity the investment company tried to contact her to reinvest the capital and interest but couldn't find her. She received a letter that had been following her around for five months. It rather curtly said 'We've been trying to contact you and you haven't been co-operating and haven't responded to our letters, so we are forced to enclose herewith a cheque for $1,147.00, which is your capital and the interest accrued over this period of years.'

We went back to the owner of the stone building and paid the rent for a year. He said, 'Yea, I knew you had money!'

God led us in those early days not to make any appeals for money. I think we needed confirmation in our own hearts that God was in this, and it wasn't just two old maids showing the world! For the first twenty years in Mafraq, we very carefully followed that policy, but now we tell our needs to those who ask.

In 1966 Roy Gustafson brought a group of tourists to Beirut and asked me to speak to them about our plans. We'd started to accept patients but were in a bare house, with no cupboards, and no nothing, just bare walls. Among those tourists was a man in his mid-fifties, whose wife had just died, and whose family had encouraged him to go on the tour. After they returned to the States Lester Gates wrote to us and said, 'I haven't been trained to do anything, but I think I can build cupboards better than you ladies can so I'll come for six months, at my own expense.' Lester came for six months in 1966 and stayed for twenty-two years as an unpaid volunteer! He built our hospital — the main building, the bomb shelter and the maintenance building.

God not only provided our financial need, but also people that he'd specially chosen and prepared to come and help us. During the 6-day war, the Iraqi army came to help in Jordan. Lester was expelled by the army for five months for being a spy because one day they caught him with a dangerous weapon. It was a little broken knife he was using to cut open a watermelon. In those days they were very anti-West and passionately hated America.

On one occasion, coming back from a town up in the north and driving a pickup truck that Lester had brought from America with him, the Iraqi soldiers flagged me down and arrested me because they said I'd been taking photos of their placements all around Mafraq. As the soldiers who did the arresting were little boys, I was incensed and said in Arabic, 'I need to see the commander of this whole unit right now!' They responded, 'You can't.'

Somebody asked, 'What does she want?' And they replied, 'She wants to see Ahmed.' I now had his name! So I said to this officer, 'I need to see Ahmed now!' 'You know him?' I responded, 'I'll know him if I see him.' So I got in but there was much aggression. I asked them if they knew what we took photos of. They all had their pencils out and were writing it down. I said, 'The chests of patients who have tuberculosis.'

When I met with Ahmed he asked what my problem was. I was furious and said, 'These soldiers have accused me of something very false and I won't tolerate this!' He replied that I couldn't do much about it. (I think, when you get angry, you often forget to be wise, and I was angry with them for wasting my time. I'd been sitting there for *hours*.) He asked, 'Who brought you here?' And I replied, 'God Almighty brought me here and nothing you can do in this world can stop him keeping me here.' He asked why I was so sure. So I shared my testimony with him and told him why I was sure God had brought me and was going to take care of me. His response was, 'You know, we could shoot you and get rid of you, and nobody would ever know where you are!' But I told him, 'No you couldn't. You couldn't touch me until God says you could, and if he says it's OK, that's all right.' 'You mean, you're not afraid of me?' he queried.

The Iraqi soldiers flagged me down and arrested me

It is a tearing wrench when they go home

I was scared but said, 'I'm not afraid of you!' My heart was beating! He looked at me for a long time and he sent all the soldiers out. Then he said, 'I'm going to tell you something.' I thought he was going to sentence me to whatever! He continued, 'I studied in Tennessee, and while I was there some born-again believers took me home and took care of me — they were trying to 'save' me but they never did. In respect to those people I'm going to let you go. Just like you said, God put me here to get you free.'

I arrived home shaking, and started to cry and everybody said, *'What happened? What happened?'* 'Nothing!' I replied. They thought I'd been tortured or something terrible had happened to me. I think many times we are not aware of how God is protecting us, but every now and then he lets us see.

That family in Tennessee probably thought they hadn't got far with this man, but under God, they're the reason I am still here today. God used that occasion in their lives. I believe things like that are happening all the time and we're not even conscious of them. Every now and then God lets us see, 'Hey, I'm still in control. It's all right.'

In 1973, after eight years, we left the rented building and moved into the present hospital building we call the Annoor Sanatorium. We registered forty beds with the Government and although we can squeeze in more we like to keep it small because we want the patients to feel they're in a family and not an institution. I love taking care of acutely ill patients and babies. Many times I wished I had trained as a doctor but as Eleanor always said, 'We didn't need two doctors when we started. We needed a nurse to head up the nursing programme and God knew what he was doing.'

Everybody here calls me 'Dockturah'. I do diagnostic work in the clinic and anybody who wears white has got to be a doctor. I used to fight it but now I think, if it makes them feel happy to call me Dockturah that's all right. I love children and, being single, I've never had any of my own but I have fostered nine orphaned Bedouin children. We keep them for about three years until they are able to survive in the desert. It is a tearing wrench when they go home because we get so attached to the little wretches! In the early days, until we got our residence, we lived in the hospital with the patients, and so for fifteen years I always had a baby in a box beside my bed.

As far as evangelism is concerned, we have five meetings a week in the wards. They're segregated by sexes, as it's culturally acceptable for the women to be separated from the men. Nasri, our male nurse, is a very valuable man to whom God has given a great love for the Bedouins and a great gift of communicating the gospel. He does most of the preaching in the men's ward and at the moment and I do most of it in the women's ward. We sing the Scripture to their own tunes — it's very discordant — I think they're tone deaf but they've got lots of rhythm so they really clap and have a good time. We then *simply* explain what the Lord Jesus has done in our lives. If you *push* Christianity, it makes them bristle but if you make it personal, they are more receptive.

Being a chronic diseases hospital, we're not rushed off our feet. The clinics are busy in the morning but most afternoons it is possible to sit for a couple of hours with the patients and get to know them. They're very curious about Christianity and ask a lot of questions. It's great just being able to meet them *at the level of their need* on a one-to-one basis. We use Scripture a lot and all those who can read get a Bible or a New Testament.

The Bedouin people have been Muslim ever since the beginning of Islam, which is 1,300 years old and they are very *proud* people, rather arrogant and a little bit sorry for everybody who isn't a Bedouin! We found, underneath that proud exterior, a very warm loving group of people.

Eleanor and I were especially concerned and burdened for them because we could see that, socially, in the Middle East, they are at the bottom of the ladder. Spiritually they have never been reached with the good news that we know is God's plan for everybody to hear. So, as two women, it was quite a challenge to come into the Bedouin world but a wonderful privilege to be able to be the first people to enter these tribes, through medicine and nursing, with the message of salvation.

We believe the Bible where it says that somebody from every tribe is going to be in heaven. We are convinced that of the fifteen major Bedouin tribes and about eighty sub-tribes that we've contacted through the hospital, there will be somebody from all of those almost one hundred tribes with us in heaven when we get there.

During the time I've been in Jordan, more than forty-five years, I've had amazingly good health. I think I've been exposed to all the bugs around the country and so am probably resistant to all the local diseases. It was quite shocking when I was in Australia fifteen years ago to be diagnosed as having cancer. I think for the first time in my life I faced my own mortality, but it was treatable with surgery and chemotherapy, and I learned through that experience the concern of believers who didn't even know me. I remember one pastor whom I had never met coming to visit every day. He was a caring man from a different denomination and we spent time every day just talking about the Lord. After I was discharged from the hospital, he took me to his church where several of the pastors prayed for my healing. I believe that God in his sovereign overruling answered their prayer and used the surgery and chemotherapy. I believe very strongly that God does answer prayers for healing. He doesn't always heal, but it's wonderful to see what he can do in answer to believing prayer.

A few years ago during Ramadan, we'd been visiting a lady who was terribly poor and had fifteen children. We had taken some clothes and things and were coming home when a speeding Volvo hit our small Lancer. For the first time in my life I was completely dependent on people.

I was in bed for four months and this was a different experience for me having been on the other side of the bed all my adult years. During this time I learned a lot about love, self-sacrificing love, through Eleanor — she was there, day and night, whenever I needed her.

I had multiple fractures and I'd barely turn over before she'd be up to see if I was OK. Eleanor was my best friend and I learned *a lot* from her. She was fourteen years older than I was but even though we were very different personalities, and we used to have some wonderful arguments, that *basic friendship* was never disturbed. She was a *faithful* friend, completely loyal, and many times I would say, 'This isn't going to work' and she'd say, 'It's gonna work! And you'd better just accept the fact that it's gonna work!' And it usually did!

She was appalled in 1991 when it was suggested that she retire. At that time a princess from the Jordanian Royal Family whom we'd got to know through Bedouin work, asked us if we'd open a clinic in the south. I replied that we didn't have the personnel. Eleanor said, 'I can do that!' So, at the age of seventy-four Eleanor went south to a new clinic. A short time after her return in 1997 she had a fire in her apartment, was overcome by the fumes and died. I guess it's like losing a spouse. We were so close and shared *everything* — when we had nothing we did it together, and when we had things, we shared them. It continues to be very difficult and I miss her *very* much.

When I look back after all these years of being on the mission field, even after receiving 'The Queen's Medal' for services in the nursing world from Queen Noor of Jordan (the wife of King Hussein) and 'The Order of Australia' for services to international relations through medical missionary work, I see the *utter faithfulness* of God. He does answer prayer.

For the first time in my life I faced my own mortality

AILEEN COLEMAN

I want to spend time with them, to sit in the dust . . .

Though many times he didn't do what *we thought* he should, nevertheless with hindsight we can always see how wonderfully he provided for or answered our needs. We found (when I say we, I'm talking about Eleanor and I — I still talk in the present tense) that we seldom had to pray for the funds to run the hospital. We didn't know where it would come from or how it would come and it was wonderful to be so relaxed about needs. Some of the new kids that come, think, *'Ah!* What's going to happen now!' But this is something that the Lord taught Eleanor and me, that if you're doing God's work, it's *his* job to take care of it — not for us, but for his glory.

I spend a lot of my prayer time praying about my own attitude, because we old women get set in our ways and we like people to do things our way! So I pray that God will help me change with the changing times, and yet never change what I've learned about his faithfulness.

Sometimes I go back to mission conferences and talk to somebody who's been in Brazil where they start a church practically every other week and I think, 'Oh, my word! We count our believers on fingers!' but I've learned over the years, and I'm still learning, that God doesn't ask for success. He asks for faithfulness and my prayer for myself is that I'll be faithful to the end.

Working in a Muslim country has a special kind of oppression and missionaries need to realise that, humanly speaking, we're not a success story. We can't talk about numbers or churches and are very aware as we come into the country, that we are a tiny minority and not wanted by the Government. We are rejected by most of the people because of what we teach, tolerated by some, loved by very few. When I return to Jordan after being in the West I'm always aware of this feeling of oppression that I know is from Satan, who is trying to discourage and cause the *op*pression to become *de*pression. But he hasn't won so far and I know he won't.

The Muslim society is a very conservative society and there are some things about Islam that are very good, it's not all evil. I've learned to appreciate a lot, not the theology of Islam, but the culture. When in the West I'm always shocked to see the state of undress of a lot of women and the lowering of moral standards, even among believers. I also see materialism, extravagance and the waste that goes on. It really distresses me to think that I know families who are practically living on bread and tea — that's their life — and I realise that if I lived in the West I'd probably get sucked into that environment. But, I find it hard to see materialism and the importance of *things*.

God has sent us some great missionary nurses so I feel that I can be released from work inside the hospital. I'll keep 'hands on' with the evangelism and plan to go out with the Bedouins. God has given us a lovely 4 x 4 car and some other churches have provided me with equipment for desert life so I can stay with them. Like an older sister, I want to spend time with them, to sit in the dust where they sit, and to share what they've got. I want to encourage the followers of the one we love. And be able to remind those that aren't, but have heard, about the things they've heard whilst they were in the hospital.

I'm getting old now, I don't want to fade away, disgruntled or discouraged, and I've never been that way. I do get discouraged; don't think I'm an angel on cloud nine! I'm very human; I lose my cool like everybody else! But in general, to *finish well* — that's what I want to do.

Jesus is my life. He gives me a reason to be on earth and gives me great joy in reaching out to people, because before I became a believer I didn't care about people — they could drop all round me and I'd think, well, what's their problem! But he's given me compassion from his heart and I can't imagine being able to exist if he weren't a part of my life, weren't the motivation, the encouragement in everything I do.

I come from a passionate Methodist holiness background and I learnt to love Jesus very, very early in life. I have images of adults with tears streaming down their faces, praying for renewal and for the transformation of the world. To see people, when you're a kid, pouring out their hearts for the world with a sense of Jesus' love, is hard to erase.

How could I tell them I didn't believe any more?

My first conversion (I have to say my first because I'm a weak person whom God has had to reconstruct many times) would have been when I was around four-and-a-half years of age. I *knew* there was naughtiness. People try to say, from a Freudian point of view, that is neurotic, but the great child psychiatrist from Harvard, Robert Coles, has kicked the stuffing out of that kind of theory. One of the most outstanding academics in his field, he states that little children often have a great sense of morality and, by the time they've finished High School, we've knocked it out of them! I felt an intense sense of what was naughty, I just cried out to God, and that was the beginning of a long pilgrimage.

Life was not easy. When I was about five years of age boiling water was accidentally poured over a large part of my body and I battled in hospital to survive the third degree burns for about five months. I was run over by a police car when I was in Primary School and at eleven or twelve years old I was hospitalised for nearly two years with Rheumatic Fever. This was during the vital socialisation period of my life so it is strange that I'm a people person. They were lonely years and much of my teens were spent going up into the mountains of Gippsland with my little pet dog.

While attending Teachers' College I briefly lost my faith. A lot of my Christian friends found it hard to believe because I was a closet atheist. That is like a Christian among a lot of atheists who are his friends; he never talks much about Jesus because he doesn't want to look a fool. Well, it was the opposite for me. The few friends I had were Christians, so how could I tell them I didn't believe any more? They would have considered me a moral leper. The church in those days didn't cope very well. Nowadays when you meet an unbeliever, they are not seen as an enemy any more, but as a friend on a journey and you just want to love them, embrace them and bring them in. But in those days you were regarded as a pariah if you pulled out, and it was tough.

I considered leaving college to get a job as a cowboy or a jackeroo, and just drink, have sex and live an analgesic lifestyle. I'd tried hard and God hadn't overcome me and made me be what I wanted to be, so I concluded that either God didn't like me, or my increasing new set of college friends who were nihilists and unbelievers were right — there was no God. My self-esteem was so low that it was easier to believe there was no God, rather than face the awful possibility that God didn't like me!

I remember the cool starry night in winter when I made that choice. Certain encounters with nature produce extremes; the Psalmist says, 'When I consider your heavens, the work of your fingers . . . what is man that you are mindful of him . . . that you care for him.' So when we look at the stars as believers we feel, 'Oh, wow! Isn't it wonderful!' But in Matthew Arnold's poem *Dover Beach*, he watches the waves incessantly rolling in and gives the nihilistic view that there's no meaning to anything. And nature suddenly gives a totally different message.

One day I preached a savage sermon . . .

So that night, nature put nails into the coffin of my hope. I looked at the stars and it all looked so immense! A few years earlier I'd read *The Mysterious Universe* that tries to explain relativity to non-scientific minds. With all this in my mentality I said, 'When I die, I die like a dog and that's all there is to it.' There was a *terrible* darkness, a *terrible* cosmic orphan-hood. I felt that if we were only a chance product of the same forces as rusty iron and ripened corn how could there be any meaning in anything! But that of course, was the genius of God because shortly after that I had to organise an Easter camp.

I'd been one of the founders of a Christian organisation on campus so it was bizarre having to pretend, while feeling totally lost and living immorally, with nobody knowing except the girl concerned. At the Easter Camp, a fiery old holiness preacher finally got through to me. And from that day to this, although I've had doubts about everything — about every politician, every church leader, about myself, about theories of epistemology — I've never had a doubt about Jesus. I'm a questioner, a troubler, I read voraciously. I'm a doubter, an inquisitor, a searcher, but have no doubts about Jesus. After all those uncertain years, he entered my room in the wee hours of the morning, and turned the stars on. I feel secure in any situation, even in the Hells' Angels headquarters. I know intensely that there's not a president, a king, a multinational board member, who can hold a candle to Jesus of Nazareth.

I came back to the Lord with a vengeance and started to read my Bible. I went berserk, reading it right through in three months and then again in the next three months, and then every year I devoured the Scriptures. I went to the Melbourne Bible Institute because I think from childhood I'd known that if I got right with God, my life would be bringing the gospel to the world. It was a fairly natural process, particularly with the strong Brethren, missionary influence of Glenna, my then unofficial fiancée.

When I first started preaching I had a passion for Jesus and love for people, but I would say whatever I believed God needed me to say, even if they were hard words. I was a racist and believed the view held by many South Africans that black people, being cursed of God, are inferior to the whites. I believed it, but I hated it because I really had a soft heart. But I had to stand by what I had been taught. One day I preached a savage sermon against Martin Luther King. I said that he was a womanising communist planted to deceive the people of God. A man came up to me afterwards — I don't know who he was, but I thank God for him. He said to me, 'Young man, have you ever met Martin Luther King?' I said, 'No.' He continued, 'Have you ever read one of his books?' 'No.' 'Have you ever heard him preach?' 'No.' 'You haven't even read one of his books?' 'No.' He reached into his back pocket, pulled out a copy of *Strength to Love* and slapped it into my hand with the words, 'Well, shut up until you have!' That was a drastic moment for me. I took it away and I cried my way through that book!

In a few months I went through what psychologists would call a Gestalt shift in consciousness, in the same way as people's attitudes changed when they saw the picture of the little Vietnamese girl with napalm on her body, in the sixties. I dropped all my political views, all my social views, and started from bedrock to reshape my theology. God took me out of my comfort zone and shook me, lovingly, almost like a terrier takes a rag and shakes it!

My ministry began to reach out and I got swept up in the Jesus Movement. I went to America to research it and met a businessman who was running Maranatha Music. I told him why I was there and he asked if I was staying in one of the Jesus houses. When I said I was he remarked that I would find it limiting. I agreed that it was a fairly strong discipline, but necessary because of their work with addicts. He remarked that in order to investigate I needed some fluidity of movement. When he realised I had no car, he had a brand new Pontiac Fury 3 delivered from a rental company within half an hour. He gave me a credit card and told me to go anywhere in Canada, the US, Central America, for as long as I wanted, just bring back the car when I had finished with it! He had never met me before but he felt God had told him to help me!

I had an amazing journey around America seeing what Jesus was doing and God spoke to me, almost audibly. He said, 'When you go back to Australia and to the hippies, begin teaching the Book of Acts, one verse at a time.' I thought, 'A Bible Study! Wow! Maybe a discussion group, but a Bible Study? With people who had nothing to do with the church?' He said, 'You do what I tell you, and it will work out!' I started with Acts Chapter one. Before long, we had between 500 and 600 people on some nights. One evening we examined the complicated issue of prophecy. Were the evangelicals right — just shout loud, sound authoritative and thump the Bible? Were the Pentecostals right — you heard a voice from God and just repeated what you heard? Or was the more rationalistic traditional preaching tradition right — a good social application of vital passages of the Bible to the immediacy of the social situation? I said to everyone, 'I don't think tonight's study is going to be much good for people who don't have any Christian roots. Because there are rumours around town that things are happening here, some of you have come expecting to find Jesus. Tonight's study isn't going to focus on that so we have people who can counsel you and tell you exactly how to find Jesus. Before I begin the study, will you stand if you really want to get converted, you really want to find Jesus and you want your life to be really changed.' Between forty and fifty people stood and I hadn't even preached a sermon! They ranged from a businessman with an attaché case, through to a couple of gang kids who handed in switchblade knives, and also a mace and a chain!

Before long we saw between 3,000 and 4,000 young people come to Jesus overnight with stories that are difficult to believe. In my current doctorate studies everything has to be rational and proven. I didn't know what to do with what was happening in those days. One guy turned up saying that he was on a bad acid trip. And he was psychotic. He said he was hanging over the flames about to be dropped into the flames of hell but a gleaming, white, shining figure came and told him, 'Go to Canterbury Road in Bayswater. There's a man called Smith. He'll tell you how to get saved!' This man had never met me! He'd never been to that area of Melbourne! He didn't know anything about it. He came into our church and asked, 'Is there someone called Smith here?' I said, 'I am he!' And he came to Jesus! He was completely cleared of his drugs. Just transformed!

Another guy hopped around one night like a dog, on hands and feet, making horrendous haunted noises. He couldn't even articulate in language. A little group of Jesus freaks chased him across people's back gardens, to a corner where he was cowering in fear. I can't explain the look in his eyes; he looked as if he was in hell. And these beautiful converted hippies, simple in their faith but *powerful* in their belief and absolutely *oozing* love out of every pore, surrounded him and began to pray for his healing. He burst into what was quite clearly another language, his face shone, and he snapped out of a *severe* acid trip! I don't know what you feel about this type of event but I feel weird, at doctoral level, even telling such stories! But he was utterly saved in that moment and his whole demeanour changed. He just softly praised God and was absolutely transformed!

At a council meeting with clergy and the Archbishop I was asked what I was doing about 'the means of grace with respect to the many young people you're seeing converted'. And I thought, 'Gosh, I'm in trouble!' because we were already baptising and giving them communion but not at the behest of any officialdom. So I asked them, 'Well, which denomination?

I feel weird, at doctoral level, even telling such stories!

Or would this group count as an ecumenical group to plant this church and take this seriously?' Everyone looked very nervous and were like rabbits going down their burrows. One person shrugged and said, 'This is sad. We would not know how to minister to these people and the councils of the church grind and move exceeding slow and sometimes the Spirit of God moves so fast that the mother church is unable to keep up with what is happening. I don't think any of our denominations could quite cope with what's going on here. You have an apostolic calling. You just have to do it. And though we can't officially say anything, know that your brothers believe that God's hand is on you — and just do it.' So I did! In a sense, we were forced to start a little mini-denomination, which grew and grew so we built the biggest mud brick building in the Southern Hemisphere.

Eddy Pye, who had been a British motorcycle stunt rider like Evil Knievel, asked us to speak at a Baptist Youth Camp in Australia at the time when young people were coming in hoards to hear us. He said, 'Smithy, why don't you get a motorcycle? All the kids love motorcycles and you'd be great out there doing that!' I laughed at him at first and then several things all happened at once. I met some young Christians, who were not very theologically astute, but were trying to form a Christian motorcycle club. I experienced one of those 'mission from God' feelings that require me to do something. I saw some outlaws by the side of the road tinkering with their bikes and downing a few beers. I knew I'd never get them into church; I had to go to them. I started to pray for them, and it was as if God said, 'Why don't you answer your own prayers?' So I got a motorcycle and we started The Christian Motorcycle Association. There is a worldwide movement with this name but we have nothing to do with it. We abandoned the name because we thought it was too middle class and conservative. A group in Sydney had been watching an old TV series called *Mod Squad*, when someone came up with the idea '*God Squad*'! And so it was formed.

It's a club that specifically reaches the tough outlaw scene. It has very strict disciplines and takes at least twelve months of riding intensely with the group to get your patch. Joining the group is a big commitment and there are expectations concerning what you are going to do. A lot of young offenders gravitate to our guys partly because of their appearance, partly because a lot of them have been there, done that, partly because of the motorcycles, partly because of the fact that these guys are street-wise and you can't pull the wool over their eyes. I think the biggest reason it is a success is that *God has pulled it together*.

To try and get Christians involved in a ministry on motorcycles and to expect some kind of discipline and accountability, was asking for a total miracle. It's the most anarchistic sub-culture, even though theoretically, it works as a tight unit, and to get even Christians with that kind of mentality to work together is really hard. But I believe it works, not because it was a 'good' idea, which it actually isn't, but because it's a *God* idea!

So much developed from that. A young guy we met in prison years ago was very impressed with the Squad and that eventually led him to Christ. He is now, I am proud to say, my son-in-law, with a gorgeous little family of five. He's become almost a nemesis to Government and those who would exploit the poor. Deeply committed, and coming from that kind of background, he understands it. A tough guy — just about as tough walking into a bureaucrat's office in Government headquarters as he would be with the kids on the street

He has set up a network of ministries like Light Path, which takes young car thieves, teaches them mechanics, and gets them permanent jobs in the motor industry. There's a group called Steps Ministry where a very adventurous woman, who has quite a sizeable family herself, has become a champion for the kids on the street. She is out all hours, in all sorts of

Smithy, why don't you get a motorcycle?

places with them. We have another programme called Inside Out dealing with kids when they come out of prison. We guarantee that twenty-four hours a day, seven days a week, if they're in trouble, if they call into the police station, if they're in a fight on the street etc they can ring a pager number and one of our staff will go to them wherever they are, which isn't the way social workers respond. As a result they respect our guys and know that they're loved. We also have Values for Life which is an attempt to take the message of Jesus — a message of real values — into the schools in a way that is not offensive to people. I've been to nearly four thousand High Schools in our country and there has been a huge impact among thousands of young people who have later found faith. We don't make appeals in class because we don't believe that would be ethically right.

We've planted churches that still tend to be on the fringe. Not because we think God is any less interested in the managing director of a large corporation — the problem is not on God's side, the problem is that the more things we have, the more there is between us and reality. Therefore it tends to be that the poor and humble spirit finds God and a poor and humble spirit usually occurs when people are powerless and marginalised. For that reason I see it as a statement of the gospel against the paradigms of power, privilege and possession that now *rule* the world — against the utilitarianism that is basic to market forces. I've raised a flag in my life for the marginalised — not because I wouldn't love to lead a Harvard professor or a multinational company director to Christ — all of that would be wonderful — but I believe in this day and age that the Good News comes more obviously to a 'nothing' person on the edge of society. To hear that Jesus loves you as much as he loves the Prime Minister or a President is wonderful.

I'm in a class struggle; I'm not trying to make a Marxist version of the gospel. But I do believe that by and large, the utilitarian philosophy in our world has led us to think that right has a lot to do with might, privilege and power. I don't want to sidetrack from the real issue of Jesus, but I want churches to beware treating Jesus like the latest supermarket to meet their needs. That's not real relationship. We need to watch that prosperity doesn't rip apart the gospel. If we have an economic collapse, it's going to be interesting to see what happens to the churches that have told us that being Godly means being wealthy. If we know the gospel, we'll love our neighbour. I would say that if we really know the gospel, and there's an economic collapse, those who have will do as they did in the first century of the church — they will make sure their brothers and sisters who don't have are cared for. That's where it will show itself in reality. I'm a social radical. I support all sorts of issues and have been in prison in the Philippines over a human rights issue. I would die for the aboriginal people, if that were necessary to take a stand for them to have land rights. If I lived in America for long I would be involved with the whole business of the Native American culture. All of that is true. But my passion is Jesus. I love him. Because there is simply no-one else!

It's going to be interesting to see what happens to the churches

Acknowledgements

This book could not have been produced without the help of so many people. I want to acknowledge, with deep gratitude, their contributions to my life and work.

A special thank you goes to all the people in this book for their time, hospitality, and going the extra mile. You are all very dear to me and I count it a privilege to know you:

To Louise, my longsuffering wife, who managed so well in my absence and has seen me eat, live and sleep this book! No easy task!!! Thank you for supporting me Louise, and keeping me on my toes:

To Sarah, Grace and Elsa, my beautiful daughters, whom I love dearly; you provide me with so much joy:

To my mother, Elsie, you always loved, encouraged and prayed for me . . . a wonderful heritage. Thank you:

To my PA, Sally Rees, who handled my correspondence and travel, and faithfully transcribed my interview tapes. Sally, you have played a key role. I would have been lost without you:

To Pauline Pearce, my prayer secretary, her husband Mike, her team and all who have prayed for this book, thank you for your friendship, enthusiasm and faithfulness. We know that prayer changes things. One day we will know just how much:

To Sylvia and Bill Pledge, my always positive and loving sister and brother-in-law:

To the Wednesday night group, thank you for supporting me in so many ways:

To Lindsay Armishaw; Douglas Balfour; Nikki and Nick Ball; Glen and Connie Balzer; Monty and Rosemary Barker; Pat Bennett; Paul Berg; Liz Block; Michael Bothamley; Becky Brettell; Caroline Cassidy; Marco Cazzulini; the church family at Christ Church, Clifton; Garry and Melissa Clark; Ross Cobb; Silas Crawley; Joy Dagher; Andrew Dakin (always a wise word); Pradip and Margaret Das; Richard and Rosalyn Dean; Elia Sipan Diaz; Andrew Dow; Lana Duim; Reynard Faber (for such long-term prayer and encouragement); Gene Hattori; Karen Hill; Richard Hill; Francis Houghton; Peter Houston; Jerry Humeny; Bishop James Jones; Glynn Leaman; Chris Lyons (accountant); Cristine Mallea; Freddy Martin; John Matchett; Sarah Montgomery; Anna and John Moore; Joan Newman (a listening ear and a dear friend); Mike Newman; Stuart Orm; Luis Palau; Graeme Paris; Joseph E. Paul; Richard Pendlebury (friend, great encourager, sounding-board and third of a triplet); Rob Pengilley; Maria Elena Ruffinatti; Julia Scholz; Richard and Barbara Sheridan; Glenna Smith; Damaris Snethlage; Gill Snow; Alan Stobbs; Murray Thom; Dr John Todd; Donna Lee Toney; Berj Topalian (regular lunchtime encouragement early in the project); Ann Travers; Steve Turner; Dave Vernon; Martin Walker; Nirmala Wati; David Wavre (thank you for believing in this book and making it a reality with your team at Eagle Publishing, Roger Judd; James Ralton; Eleanor Axcell, thank you for your laughter, encouragement and such a sensitive edit. I have really enjoyed our long telephone conversations); Francis Whitehead; Alfonso Wieland.

I just know I will forget someone! Please be assured that I really appreciate all your help. I have received help from interpreters, drivers, bag carriers, encouragers, prayers, friends and family, and a stranger I met on an airline who, when I told her about the book, said, 'Please don't let this just be another picture book, make sure there is enough room for the stories.'

Last and most important, thanks go to Tim Brettell, a gracious and dear friend, whose encouragement and being there for me on a day-to-day basis throughout, has seen this project realised.